R. m

20-00

[illegible]

Neither This Nor That But . . . Aum

Other English Books
by
Nitya Chaitanya Yati

The Psychology of *Darśana Mālā*

The *Bhagavad Gīta* (Commentary)

Love and Devotion

The Haunting Echoes of Spring

A Bouquet of Verses in Praise of the Supreme Mother

Experiencing the *Īśāvāsya Upaniṣad*

The Bṛhadāraṇyaka Upaniṣad Vols. 1 and 2

Śree Narayana Guru

Daiva Daśakam (Translation and Commentary)

Psychology: An Eastern Perspective

Bhakti

Vināyakāṣṭakam (Translation and Commentary)

God: Reality or Illusion?

Prāṇāyāma

Arivu - Epistemology of Gnosis

An Intelligent Man's Guide to the Hindu Religion

Neither This Nor That But . . . Aum

One Hundred Meditations based on Narayana Guru's *Ātmōpadeśa Śatakam*

Nitya Chaitanya Yati

D.K. Printworld (P) Ltd.
NEW DELHI-110015

Cataloging in Publication Data — DK

Nitya Chaitanya, *Yati*, 1924-
Neither this nor that but . . . aum.

1. Narayana Guru, 1856-1928. Ātmōpadeśa śatakam. 2. Meditation -- Hinduism. 3. Vedānta. 4. Philosophy, Indic. I. Narayana Guru, 1856-1928. Ātmōpadeśa śatakam. English & Malayalam. II. Title.

First published in 1982
This edition 1995

ISBN 81-246-0057-0

Published and printed by :
D.K. Printworld (P) Ltd.
Regd. office : 'Sri Kunj', F-52, Bali Nagar
New Delhi - 110015
Phone: (011) 546-6019; *Fax*: (011) 546-5926

Immortality is becoming fearless.
The Absolute is fearless.
He who knows it as such
certainly becomes the fearless Absolute.

Bṛhadāraṇyaka Upaniṣad

FOREWORD

When it was first suggested that I should write an introduction to this work, I sat at my desk surrounded by reference books: biographies of Narayana Guru, other commentaries on the verses and various other relevant scholarly works. I read avidly and made many notes, then I started to write. What resulted was a scholarly piece which completely lacked conviction and was therefore meaningless. I am not a scholar, so I decided to leave the introduction to someone better equipped to do it than I. I would like to contribute to it however, in my own unscholarly way, whatever comes directly from my heart and my experience.

This work consists of one hundred verses written in Malayalam by Narayana Guru with translations and commentaries by Guru Nitya Chaitanya Yati. Its title in Malayalam is *Ātmopadeśa Śatakam,* which means: one hundred verses of Self-instruction. This is, in fact, the title of a most valuable complementary work written by Nataraja Guru, who was Narayana Guru's chief disciple and propagator of his legacy of wisdom.

Narayana Guru was a mystic, a philosopher, a visionary, a scientist and a poet all rolled into one. He is no longer physically alive, but he is very much alive in the dynamism of his vision. As I am writing I am facing a large photograph of the Guru. It is a piece of paper that gives away nothing. I do not know him as a man except through hearsay. I only know him as my essence, the essence that manifested from the dark depths of ignorance and forgetfulness during my long involvement with this work. Thus, I cannot say that I relate to Narayana Guru, the man, but I can say with utmost conviction that I am steeped in the essence that exudes from his life-work. It is this essence that I hope will guide my pen in the next few pages.

In the autumn of 1977 I was living in Portland, Oregon, U.S.A. with a small group of people whose main purpose was to find the meaning of life through Self-awareness. We were guided through this journey by Guru Nitya. He was the mirror into which we looked to find ourselves. The mirror he presented to us was unblemished, not so the reflections, however. What we saw in him depended upon our own understanding of reality. At times we enjoyed moments of great clarity, but we often surrounded ourselves with fogs that ranged from mild mists to veritable pea-soupers. It was a very intense life-situation, which for me lasted one year. During this period I experienced the densest fog imaginable—the darkest night of the soul.

I was in the wake of this dismal darkness when Guru Nitya suggested a study of *Ātmopadeśa Śatakam*. We all reacted with great enthusiasm, even though the proposal entailed getting up at 5.30 a.m. for one hundred consecutive days. At least for me this enthusiasm had nothing to do with *Ātmopadeśa Śatakam* which up to this point was nothing more than a heap of incomprehensible words. Nor was I stimulated by Narayana Guru, who then was merely a stern face in a dusty picture frame. It was Guru Nitya's enthusiasm and inner joy that made me agree to such a rigorous regime. For one hundred days, rain, shine, or snow-storm, I tracked up a steep hill in the pitch darkness of northern winter mornings to participate in Guru Nitya's meditations. Each morning he dealt with a new verse. Our discipline consisted of living out the teachings for that day, keeping the verse in mind throughout our daily transactions. We then met again in the evening and, if inclined to, we discussed our reactions to it, our perceptions and the way we applied it to common-place events of our daily existence. We started as a small group, but it quickly grew in size till it filled our large common-room to capacity. People came from all parts of Portland, many travelling many miles in all weather conditions.

The first meditation was sublime. I fell into a trance-like state and I was not aware of the meaning of the words I was hearing. Words came and went independently of each other. I reemerged from this state with a feeling of weightlessness, though I soon felt intellectually frustrated as I could not recall anything. The entry in my journal that day reads:

> A new day, new directions. Nitya has initiated a new regime. I feel tearful, though not emotional. I cannot rationalize this feeling. I could say they are tears of gratitude, but that would confine something that feels far greater. Verse one has been in mind all day and each time I try to apply it consciously to an experience or a thought, I find I have already done so unconsciously. And it feels so right, as though I had been born to it.

I did not know it then, but I was born to it. Between frequent lapses, I had unconsciously lived within the framework of Narayana Guru's vision of the Absolute all my life.

I am convinced that every human being is born with the legacy of this universal vision. It is our only real inheritance. Few, however, are the people who do not succumb to the veiling of reality caused by our emotional and sensory experience of life. I was one of the many that succumbed. I had reached a point where all my energy was directed at pitting myself against life, and I could no longer conceive life as that greatest of gifts that it is.

For one hundred days I was totally steeped in *Atmopadeśa Śatakam*. Each verse caused an inner turmoil, and although each turmoil seemed different, I can now see that the pattern was the same throughout. The day would start blissfully, with a feeling of total abandonment, as I surrendered all my thinking power and I passively absorbed Guru Nitya's words. This was followed by panic, when I came to realize that I had not digested anything intellectually. The panic remained with me until some perception or experience which I would normally pass off as common-place would acquire a new depth of significance. This brought about a sense of excitement. Then slowly, as excitement waned, I would start to flash back to thoughts and deeds of my childhood and early youth when I had had similar insights. In my childhood such insights were common, though I was not conscious of any particular value attached to them. It was just my way of perceiving life.

As life unfolds its unpredictable path it deals many blows, and as we grow older, the feeling of self-pity and delusion that each blow educes grows and grows. In self-protection we build armours around ourselves to fend off the next blow, but fate, sneaky fellow that he is, always hits us unexpectedly below the belt. Thus, we strengthen our armours till we forget what it feels like to live free of self-defences and illusions. The memory of freedom scatters into oblivion.

I needed the jolt of *Ātmopadeśa Śatakam* to reawaken those scattered memories and to assemble them into a whole cohesive vision. The process that I underwent each day became quite torrid at times. I often balked at some of the memories it reawakened, because, in the course of time, I had moved to the opposite pole of the particular value they denoted and it can be very painful to demolish an edifice so carefully constructed over a long period. The more comfortable and pleasurable the edifice is, the more painful the demolition. *Ātmopadeśa Śatakam* pushed on however.

There was no time to dwell on phantoms. Each new verse brought about its own set of demolition programmes that had to be dealt with.

After three or four weeks of this regime, I became aware that Nitya was writing something in Malayalam. It was a concise rendition of the morning meditations. I became fascinated with this because I would dearly have loved to read the essential core of all the words that I had not assessed during the morning discourse. I suggested he should translate it and I should type it. He firmly refused. I insisted. He refused. I insisted some more. He finally agreed, though reluctantly. For once, my pig-headedness brought me joy. I am grateful to him beyond words for taking on the extra chore of dictating his translations, because while I worked on them I was forced to assimilate conceptually what could otherwise have been indolently left to the purely perceptual stage.

As I became more and more deeply committed, I began to realize that not only were my forgotten memories reawakened, but I was also being presented with a vision of cosmology that I had never even vaguely envisioned before. Not only was I helped in the arduous task of scaling the central stem of the mighty tree of knowledge, but I was also shown even the frailest twig at the tip of every branch and the flimsiest root tendril reaching far underground. It took three years to get the script ready for publication. During these three years I have had the opportunity to revise and actualize every perception I had during the original one hundred days and to become aware of the perceptions that I had missed the first time around. No doubt I will be able to say the same in years to come.

One could say that I have lived each word in this book to the full. They ring in my ears, they tickle my mind, they slide off my tongue and they fill my heart to capacity. This is the sublime vision of Narayana Guru transmitted through the sublime vision of Guru Nitya and rendered in his words, yet each word is absolutely mine by absorption. These words have been, are and always will be the essential core of every moment of my life. Every verse is as perfect and complete as a rare pearl, and these perfect pearls are linked by the golden thread of pure essence, which is my essence, your essence, our inheritance.

Mankind is occasionally graced by the presence in its midst of a rare human being who not only enjoys an unclouded vision of reality, but has also the means to transmit it to his fellowman. He is the eternal beacon in the terrifying darkness of ignorance. Narayana Guru is such a being and *Ātmopadeśa Śatakam* is his ever radiating beam.

Earlier I described a photograph of Narayana Guru as a piece of paper that gave away nothing. Unwittingly I defined essence. It gives away nothing, nor does it take away anything. It is the spinal fluid of our existence and it is also the amniotic fluid in which our existence unfolds. We at once contain it and are contained by it. We are it.

Neither that, nor this, nor the meaning of existence am I,
but existence, consciousness, joy immortal; thus attaining clarity,

emboldened,
discarding attachment to being and non-being,
one should gently, gently merge in *SAT-AUM.*

(Verse 100)

EDDA WALKER

AUTHOR'S NOTE

In the autumn of 1977, the students of the Narayana Gurukula, Portland, Oregon, USA, committed themselves to one hundred days of meditation, which were held both in the mornings and in the evenings. Each day attention was focussed on the purport of one verse from Narayana Guru's main mystical composition, *Ātmopadeśa Śatakam.* Each verse was taken sequentially.

In the mornings students listened to the meaning of the commentary of a verse and in the evenings, gatherings were held to share the experiences of living the Guru's instruction for each day.

During the period of this session, the gist of it was prepared to make two handy books, one in Malayalam and one in English. This comprehensive text, containing the meaning of the hundred verses and the main guidelines for meditation, was prepared with the earnest cooperation of Edda Walker. A similar book in Malayalam has already been published.

The name of the present book *Neither This Nor That But...Aum* is derived from the one hundredth verse of *Ātmopadeśa Śatakam.* In fact, the 99 verses that precede it clearly explain the "This" and "That" in which our life becomes entangled. As we proceed from verse to verse, we are told with the untold magic of the silent Word the secret of supreme realization.

NARAYANA GURU

Today everybody speaks of one world, one humanity, of the essential unity of religion, and of the irrevocable solidarity of mankind. But one hundred years ago, when Narayana Guru presented his ideal of man as "one in kind, one in religion and one in God," the people who listened to him were not the masses who have been "massaged" by Marshall McLuhan's media. Narayana Guru's audience was the neglected, hated, hunted and tabooed pariah, who saw in him a ray of hope for the persecuted masses of the world that toiled and moiled in sunshine and rain to feed, clothe and fatten those high-ups in the society whose prerogative it was, in turn, to sin against man's dignity and compassion.

Narayana Guru was born in a South Indian village which had the heritage of one of the eight "Pillais" who challenged the regal right of the Prince of Tiruvancode and set the precedent of thwarting the social status quo. Further, he was born not long after the first shots were fired in 1857 by the ranks of the Indian army which rose against the British hegemony in India. Thus, the psychological augury which symbolized the time of Narayana Guru's birth later became significant in Indian history as the mark of a radical outbreak of the counterblast of India's masses which began to question every authority and sanction that gave its approval to the tyranny of injustice.

From the first hymn of the *Ṛg Veda* which extolls the benevolence of fire, to its final deception which buries the denominator basis of Indian society in the mire of untouchability, what had been going on within the labyrinth of Indian social intrigues was studied and scrutinized by the Guru in the best light of India's highest wisdom, cherished by the *Upaniṣads*, the *Kural* and *Thevaram*. He confronted Manu's concept of righteousness and social justice with his own firm stand on the dignity of man and adherence to Truth, and he challenged the wholesale injustice perpetuated by the *Dharma Sastras* (Hindu ethical codes) and theocracy by revaluing *dharma* in his teachings and by exemplifying with his own life the all-embracing mode of a *brahmavit*. He lived with the caring benevolence of a compassionate Buddha and a loving Jesus. He set the pace of the new revaluation with personal examples, such as giving the pariah a chance to live the highest ideals of the *Upaniṣads*, and eschewing all differences of caste and creed by opening places of worship and education where every man could assemble, work, learn and live in fraternity.

From dust he made men of dignity who became resourceful as leaders in all walks of life and who gave literature a new tilt and meaning to trumpet the message of social, political and economic change. In Narayana Guru's campaign against caste taboos, Mahatma Gandhi personally attended and offered the historical *satyagraha* (passive resistance) at Vaikom. Gurudev Tagore of Santiniketan found in the Guru at Sivagiri the most ancient of ṛṣis reliving the wisdom of *Advaita* without debasing its tenets by using them as polemic ideals against anybody's spiritual or philosophical vision.

Narayana Guru was born in Chempazhanti, near Trivandrum, in 1854 and he passed away in September 1928 at Varkala, Kerala. His works are mainly written in Sanskrit, Malayalam and Tamil. The most popular among these works is *Ātmōpadeśa Śatakam* (One Hundred Verses of Self Instruction), of which the present work is a carefully close translation into English.

NITYA

GUIDE TO MALAYALAM PRONUNCIATION

The sounds indicated in the examples are only approximations of the original Malayalam sounds. Besides vowels only those consonants which represent sounds more or less alien to the English language are listed.

Vowels

a	pronounced like the u in "but"
ā	like the a in "far"
i	like the e in "me"
ī	a longer sound, like the ee in "beet"
u	like the o in "to"
ū	a longer sound, like the oo in "pool"
ṛ	like the ri in "rig" (very short)
e	like the a in "gate"
ai	like the i in "high"
ō	like the o in "note"
au	like the ou in "loud"

Consonants

n	pronounced as the n in "China"
ṭ	as the t in "got"
ṭṭ	compound of ṭ as in "butter"
n	close to the ny in "symphony"
ṟ	pronounced as the r in "ran"
ṟṟ	close to the t in "it"
ṅ	pronounced as the ng in "sing"
c	pronounced as the ch in "chunk"
ñ	as the n in spanish "Señor"
ññ	compound of ñ
t	sound close to the th in "blithe"
th	close to the th in the name "Othello"
dh	as the dh in "dharma"
l	pronounced as the l in "love"
ḷ	pronounced as the l in "play"
ś	pronounced as a gentle sound like in the German word "deutsch"

ṣ	pronounced as the s in "she"
s	pronounced as the s in "same"
ẓ	between the s in "pleasure" and the j in the French name "Jean"

Verse 1

aṟivilumēṟiyaṟiññiṭunnavan ta-
nnuruvilumottu puṟattumujjvalikkum-
karuvinu kaṇṇukal añcumuḷḷaṭakki-
tterutere vīṇu vaṇaṅṅiyōtiṭēṇam.

In and beyond the knowledge which shines
at once within and without the knower
is the *karu*; to that, with the five senses withheld,
prostrate again and again with devotion and chant.

This verse ends with the word "chant." In India the Vedas are honoured as the most authentic scriptures for worshipful chanting. It is the intention of Narayana Guru that this work should be used in the same manner. *Ātmopadeśa Śatakam* is meant to be both a book of instructions and a song to sing.

The word *karu* refers to the Supreme Being which seems to be in a process of eternal becoming or continuous manifestation. When our eyes are open we see things, people and events. On all such occasions, ideas such as "I" and "mine" arise and also differentiations such as "not I" and "not mine." From such kind of ideation mind should be turned again and again to the Supreme Being with this prayer:

> My Lord, you are all this. You are the one who is shining as this universe. I am seeing you as children, as grown-ups, as myself and others. Again and again I forget that you are everything. Because of this forgetfulness I become arrogant and aggressive, indifferent and irreverent. As I am not watchful of your all-seeing eyes, lapses occur and I indulge in untruths. Oh Lord, bless me. Open my eye of wisdom. When children play, may I have eyes to see your loving and caring look in the eyes of everyone. In every sound that vibrates in my ears, let me hear the sweetness of your voice. Instead of feeling that I am an individual, let there prevail the consciousness of the totality in all its wholeness. May I always have a sense of being inseparable from the whole. May this prayer always echo in the

horizon of my mind. Help me repeat this verse and go deeper and deeper into the wonder of its meaning, and may I feel the blessedness of this unitive comprehension. *Aum....*

Verse 2

karaṇavumindriyavum kaḷēbaram to-
ṭṭaṟiyumanēka jagattumōrkkil ellām
paraveḷi tanniluyarnna bhānumān tan-
tiruvuruvāṇu tiraññu teṟiṭēṇam.

The inner organ, the senses, the body,
the many worlds known by direct perception – everything, when contemplated,
is the glorious embodiment of the sun that shines in the sky beyond;
this should be known through relentless search.

In deep sleep we do not know anything. When darkness recedes and the eastern horizon slowly becomes clear, light returns. In the same way, when we wake, consciousness returns. Several questions arise in the mind then, such as: "Is it morning already? What could the time be now? Should I get up now? What are the things to be done today?" The wakeful state is replete with such questions.

The questioning aspect of our consciousness is called *manas*. These questions evoke memories, and relevant memories are relived in a new form in the experience of the present.

Memories that give meaning to an experience are called *cittam*. These memories also bring along with them the idea of values. In the light of such recalled values, mind judges the significance of everything presented to it. The faculty that is used for judging is called *buddhi*.

"It is already 6 o'clock." "I should get up." "The children must go to school." "I should help them." In all such decisions there is something definitive about our will. It also indicates how a situation becomes affective. We become conscious of our personal identity and we will not be happy if we cannot carry out our will. This aspect of personal identity is called *ahaṁkara*. The questioning aspect of the mind, its recall of memory, decision making, and the personal sense of affectivity and identity come under the blanket phrase *antaḥkaraṇa*, or inner organ.

At the core of our consciousness there is an unchanging constant.

We relate all our sensations, feelings, thoughts and every kind of experience to this core which is recognized as the I—consciousness.

Each time the inner organ becomes active, it begins to use the five organs of perception. The organs of perception interact with external forces such as light, sound and various kinds of pressures. Our sensory experiences are mainly tactual; there are pleasurable contacts and painful contacts. As we use all the five sense organs and mind for a meaningful relationship with the external world, we combine the data received from the different senses and make meaningful compositions to constitute each unit of experience. In every experience of the external world there is the coming together of an inner sense of value and an outer world of interrelated things which are expressive of that value. When the inner sense of value and its outer manifestation are taken together as a whole, it is called *lokam*. In our every-day life we go from one *lokam* to another.

In the darkness of night nothing is seen, but when the sun rises we see trees, lawns, sky, people and all sorts of other things. All these objects of perception were there before they were revealed by the sunlight. In fact, we see only the sunlight. Because of the contrast between light and shadow, shapes are projected. For every familiar shape we have assigned some name. The visible world is nothing but a study of light and shade. In the same manner, our Self should be considered as analogous to the sun; it is shining in the firmament of consciousness. Like light and shadow, we have knowledge and ignorance as the contrasting elements in the field of awareness. Various kinds of configurations take place within the field of consciousness and we call these perceptions, conceptions, and every form of structuring that is made of these two basic elements, "the world." In short, there is only consciousness. Everything we experience is its modulation.

What is called consciousness here is the same as the Self. The same Self is to be venerated as the Most Divine; it can be called God or the Absolute. Pure happiness is also nothing other than the one source of all knowledge.

Verse 3

veḷiyilirunnu vivarttaminnu kāṇum
velimutalāya vibhūtiyañcumōrttāl
jalanidhi tannil uyarnniṭum taraṅgā-
valiyatupōleyabhēdamāy varēṇam.

Existing outside and, as specific modes, seen within,
the five elements, like sky, when contemplated,
should become like waves rising in rows
from the treasury of the watery deep, without any separate reality whatsoever.

There is a world outside which contains things we like and things we dislike: also there are a number of things to which we are indifferent. When sleep comes all these things fade out and finally nothing is left. When we are in deep sleep we don't even know that. Next morning, when we wake, we see the sun shining in the far distance where the horizon separates the sky from the earth. We walk to the kitchen and turn on the stove; when we turn a tap, water comes and we make tea or coffee. We sit by the window and gently sip the hot drink. Cool breezes blow softly. Thus, every morning we experience the five elements: sky, air, fire, water and earth. We experience and enjoy all these things outside us. These experiences are also shared by others and we get into interpersonal relationships with ease, as it is fairly easy to refer to things outside and to exchange our views on them. From all this we easily conjecture that there is an external world out there, as we see it and experience it.

If we study physics, chemistry and physiology, the new notions derived from these sciences may shake our comfortable idea of the external world. For instance, the colour we see outside is said not to be there; what we see are only variations in the frequency of the light wave. The colour is only an interpretation of the effect of light by the chemical changes in our brain. It is surprising to know that there are no sounds outside; all the din and rattle of machines, as well as the finest of musical melodies are the exaggerated versions of an insignificant happening in the cochlea. Form is a contrast of light and shadow. It is strange that the mind can forget the variations of size if the forms are identical. The model of an elephant which is only the size of a mosquito and the model of a mosquito which is the size of an elephant will not cause any confusion of identity because of their diminutive or exaggerated sizes. After all, what are time and space other than the visualizing of the relationships of things?

Our head is not bigger than a pumpkin and the inner drama that is staged in it has an exact correspondence to what is imagined to be a universe of infinite magnitude. We conveniently presume that our inner experience is the outer world. We imagine there are others, although those outsiders are also our insiders. However, when we talk with them they do not embarrass us. Instead of them sitting and squeaking in the folds of our brain, they stand solidly outside and speak as separate identities.

If we break open a head we don't see anything other than a gray jelly, yet with it we experience a depth which is deeper than anything we can imagine. In our inspired moments we can spread the wings of our imagination and soar very high. What is this depth and where is that height? There is no greater wonder than our Self. It is appropriate that Guru calls this Self an oceanic treasury of the Divine. In Sanskrit, the ocean is called *ratnākara,* which means filled with precious stones. In the same way, the depth of our consciousness is also filled with inexhaustible bliss.

The Supreme Being is none other than the knowledge of the Self and its many manifestations, such as earth, water, fire, air and ether. Like waves arising from the ocean, modulations of consciousness rise and fall on the surface of our mind. Each such modification has its own quality which is experienced as pain or pleasure.

Sleep is a state where there are no waves of consciousness, where the individuation merges into the totality. As this is a very peaceful state, we seek to return to it when we are physically or mentally tired, but if sleep was to be the permanent termination of our world-experience, we would be frightened. When there is no body, there are no modulations of consciousness. Only when the body is animated and we are aware of our own true nature can we experience the gold crested waves of the oceanic treasury of blissful consciousness.

We should ever aspire to have that knowledge which reveals to us our inseparable identity with the Supreme Being. Only then will this world transform into a feast of continuous enjoyment.

Verse 4

ar̲ivumar̲iññiṭumartthavum pumānta-
nnar̲ivumorādi mahassu mātramākum;
viraḷataviṭṭu viḷaṅṅumammahattā-
mar̲ivilamarnnatu mātramāyiṭēṇam.

Knowledge, the objectivization of the value of the known
and one's personal knowledge are nothing other than *mahas*;
merging into that infinite supreme
knowledge, become that alone.

Wakeful consciousness is a changing phenomenon. When you see your child you think, "here is my child." This not mere imagination. The very recognition of the child produces in you a feeling that is permeated with a value of endearment; the joy of that fills your whole being from head to feet. There is an inexpressible ecstasy in that knowledge. Guru refers to that as the object of knowledge. The special word used here is *arttham.* It also means "meaning" – the meaning of what you happen to know and what you evaluate.

Thousands of interests are lying hidden as potential forces in us. These are called *vāsana*-s. Not all *vāsana*-s are pleasure-giving, some are intrinsically connected with an instinct of self-preservation. This can generate fear, a sense of insecurity, anxiety, a sense of rejection and confusions of all sorts. When any one of these potential forces comes to the surface of the mind and relates itself to an outside factor, a sense of object changes into a meaningful matter of great concern. On the one hand it creates a certain mood in the mind, and on the other hand the mind finds a counterpart to react with. In a short while, mind is freed of that situation and it merges into its normal state of the unconscious; it is ready again to hook on to another subject. When the mind prides itself in the feeling of "this is my son," the knowledge concerning "I" and the idea of "the son" merge into one, and this is experienced only as a joyous feeling. The explicit distinction of me and my son arises only when it becomes a discursive thought. What is true of the experience of happiness is also true of the experience of unhappiness.

How do all the interests come to the surface and become items of conscious experience? From the beginning of beginningless time a certain force that either resembles or is identical with intelligence and physical dynamics has been making things manifest in various forms. Animated forms are recognized as corporeal beings. Another aspect of manifestation is the culturing or breeding of latent possibilities which have within them an imperative compulsion to become actual. At the human level, these latent potentials are synonymous with what has been described as *vāsana*-s. This knowledge-like principle is identical with God for the religiously-minded person, to philosophers it is an absolute principle, and to scientists it is the primeval law of nature. This knowledge operates in the human mind by illuminating within the person his or her own desires, and outside the person, the object that is intrinsically connected with the desire. When we look at the common source of the illumination of both the subject and the object we see only the indescribable numinous glow which for convenience we call the Absolute and for irrational reasons of value significance, God. The Guru calls it here the *mahas*, the primal being. This mysterious and infinite knowledge is not only beginningless, but it is also of infinite possibility and potential.

Unfortunately most human beings are trapped in the dark caves of a few personal and private interests. If we were to become successful in giving up our private interests in favour of an altruistic benevolence, such as can be seen in the spring season, which blesses the entire vegetative world to blossom forth, we would live the glory of the all-permeating love of the Divine. In such a state the entire world becomes the counterpart of our interest.

Absolute love is described as *bhakti.* Small love, such as the infatuation for another, brings bondage. It blindfolds our capacity to see the universality of the Self. We should live with the knowledge that cancels out the subject and the object into the incessant joy which results from the harmonious coupling of being with becoming.

Verse 5

ulakar uṟaṅṅiyuṇarnnu cintaceyyum
palatumitokkeyumuṟṟupārttu nilkkum-
vilamatiyātaviḷakkudikkayum pin-
polikayumillitu kaṇṭu pōyiṭēṇam.

Worldly people, having slept, wake and think many thoughts;
ever wakefully witnessing all this shines an unlit lamp,
precious beyond words; that never fades;
ever seeing this, one should go forward.

After living in this world for some time, somehow we eventually adopt a life-style that will ultimately help us find a niche in the general setup of the world. In our mother's womb we didn't know anything. For nine months we were in a state of anesthesia, while the great artificer put all our organs together in their right places. When we came out we found the assignments given to us by nature were so tiring that again and again we reverted to our old habit of sleeping. Ultimately, waking and sleeping became our alternating pattern. In between these two states, like the twilight between day and night, we have developed the intermediary state of dreaming. The main difference between the sleeping state and the wakeful state is the operational impact of time consciousness which is experienced only in the wakeful state. It comes in the form of sequences of short and long duration beginning with the question "what next?" This is how we hook on to a new interest.

The flowering and fruition of an interest is like the unfoldment of a latent cause until the quanta of energy in it is fully dissipated in the process of its actualization. As soon as we get to the tail end of the fulfillment of an interest or the failure of its gratification the recurring question "what next?" pops up. Again we live through the whole cycle. There is no end to this. In spite of all the dramatic and traumatic changes in the actualization or the failure of each unit of interest there is always a presiding lamp impartially shedding its light on all the thematic reductions that are going on. This lamp is what the Guru refers to in the first verse as the cosmic yolk that is shining both as the world outside and the world inside, and as the supernal sun that shines in the firmament of consciousness.

In the *Bṛhadāraṇyaka Upaniṣad* and the *Taittirīya Upaniṣad* the Supreme Self is described as the eye behind the eye and the mind behind the mind. There is nothing more precious than this light which shines within us. It was there even before the individuation of our personal self commenced its manifestation in the present physical form. The same light was in our parents and was even present before the beginning of the universe. Even when everything crumbles and disappears this lamp will continue to shine, that is why it is called *daivam* – the light of all lights.

When a person says "I" that "I" contains the light of the Absolute and the shadows of the relative. This consciousness alternates between recognizing the light and forgetting it. When Kṛṣṇa advised Arjuna to be of his mind, what he meant was for him to remain ever wakeful to this eternal light. Jesus Christ exhorted his disciples to have this realization when he said, "I am the life and the light and the path and the goal." Let us take refuge again and again in this light.

Verse 6

uṇaraṇaminniyuṟaṅṅaṇam bhujiccī-
ṭaṇamaśanam puṇarēṇamennivaṇṇam
aṇayumanēka vikalpamākayālā-
ruṇaruvatuḷḷoru nirvikāra rūpam?

One has to wake up, then go to sleep,
has to eat food and embrace; thus, in this way
many ambivalent urges arise; therefore,
who is there to comprehend reality's one changeless form?

The sun rises and sets. Thus, night follows day. As life on earth is directly related to solar energy, the earth's rotations upon its axis, which cause day and night, affect the lives of all living things. Most living beings are heliotropic; they wake up and become active when the sun rises and go to sleep when the sun no longer stimulates them. In our wakeful state we engage in activities which consume energy, and to replenish the body we need food. In the course of a day we eat two or three times and we may have the craving to eat at odd hours. This body of ours is an instrument that expresses several specific functions motivated by its latent tendencies.

The whole world is an aggregate of bodies not dissimilar to ours, even though some of them look as inert as a rock that has been there for ages, or as superactive, without conscious motivation, as radium generating radon gas.

These innate potentials, whether of a metal or of a chemical or of the human mind, are collectively referred to as of *dharma.* Earth is called *dhara,* which has the same root as *dharma.* This is another indication that everything on earth is potentially of a changing order. We are as much a part of nature as earth, water or fire.

The structural details of a psycho-physical organism are ingenuous devices to produce various kinds of functions. Even a simple look at our physiological functions, such as the circulation of blood, the respiration of the lungs, or the digestion of food, can reveal to us how our body is ever as active as hundreds or thousands of mills and factories of all kinds which are kept functioning around the clock. Although most of the functions are ingenuously managed by some unknown intelligence, which for lack of understanding we assign to the unconscious, a wide range of actions also come under the direct care and supervision of our conscious mind. To keep the bodily functions going we have to relate ourselves to other bodies and other persons. From this need arises a world of transaction. The motivation of the mind has to square with the promise of values that remains explicit or implicit in the world outside with which we relate.

Thus if motivation arises from our *dharma,* our fulfillment belongs to the world of *artha,* or meaningful value. The mechanism that relates the *dharma* to the *artha,* or the latent urge to its fulfillment, is the conscious manifestation of a desire. This is called *Kāma.* Thus, the lot of the common man is to be subjected to these three natural functions which are respectively known as *dharma, artha* and *kāma.*

At a certain stage of development this pattern changes like a quantum leap. A person changes his mode of search from gratification of desires to a sharp drop of most of his desires. He yearns for relief from work. This leads him to the search for the final deliverance. As in most people energy runs out before they come to this turning point, little stamina is left to turn away from the several entanglements in the world of special functions to the changeless unity of the transcendent Being. Hardly anyone knows of even the existence of the pure Being of transcendence. In the present verse Guru deplores this sad state to which we are subjected.

Verse 7

uṇararutinniyuṟaṅṅiṭātirunnī-
ṭaṇamaṟivāyitininnayōgyanennāl
praṇavamuṇarnnu piṟappoẓiññu vāẓum-
munijana sēvayil mūrtti nirttiṭēṇam.

Do not wake anymore, and without sleeping remain as knowledge;
if you are unfit for this,
then keep yourself in the service of those contemplatives
who live free from birth, awakened to *aum*.

The Guru says: "Do not wake up." This is immediately followed by another instruction: "Without sleeping remain." There cannot be instructions more contradictory than these. How can we wake up if we are not sleeping? If we are already awake, why are we asked not to wake up? If waking up is synonymous with giving attention to the gratification of some need, what could be that need? Similarly, if sleeping is the forgetfulness of something, what is the remembrance that the Guru wants to perpetuate?

It is a biological imperative for the psycho-physical organism of a human being to have the two alternating functions of waking and sleeping. There are many autonomous functions within the body that show similar alternating patterns, such as the diastole and systole of the heart and the exhaling and inhaling of the lungs. Mind also has its own programme of ambivalence and cycles of alternating states of consciousness. The Guru is a wise man very well informed on all these psychic and physical functions of the organism; so there should be some reason for giving instructions which look so enigmatic.

The key to this verse lies in the previous one. We have already seen that all heliotropic beings wake up and become active when the sun comes up, and go to sleep when the sun is gone. When we wake up it is not just an individual waking up, but a whole host of needs of physical and mental order also wake up. The body needs water and food, and the senses show their special preferences in the items of drink and food that are to be cooked and served. The eye is willing to look at anything and the ear is willing to hear anything, but it is the mind that makes a big deal of what the senses see, hear, smell, or touch and taste. From this, it is evident that the mind plays a major role in the state of wakefulness. It becomes so totally identified with the quality of the sensory experience that it cuts itself off from the main stream of our consciousness. This was amply explained and illustrated in the previous six verses. Thus the Absolute and Transcendent Being, in their infinitude, are left behind in oblivion and the mind confines itself to a transient, worthless and trivial situation. This can be compared to the forgetfulness of identity when a person goes to sleep. The true identity of the Self is its pure state of bliss consciousness. This was previously alluded to as the supernal sun shining in the sky of consciousness, the treasury of oceanic depth and the unlit lamp that ever shines.

We enjoy our momentary infatuations at the cost of losing our soul, as it were. This is why Guru instructs us to remain without sleep. From the same example, it naturally follows that in these simple events of life our seeming wakefulness is only that of a sleep-walker who puts on the light, walks around his room, does some work like an automaton and then goes to sleep again without having the least idea of what he was doing. Such a person undeniably experiences whatever he is doing at the time of his doing it, but it is of little or no consequence for making his life meaningful or valuable.

When Guru asks us not to wake up he is only cautioning us against taking an interest in the trivialities of the sensory world. He knows pretty well, as is evident from the previous verse, all the alternations and ambivalences in an individual's life. He knows from his own experience that there is a possibility of minimizing the horizontal sharpness of wakeful infatuation and of lessening the heavy benumbing inertia of sleep, so that one can remain in a neutral position which is neither the state of wakefulness nor of sleep. The Guru is not however suggesting a state like that of reverie or day-dreaming. What he recommends here is a state of equipoise or beatitude which has all the restfulness of sleep and all the vigilance of wakefulness, and which is not bifurcated within it with the search to gratify any special need.

This ideal which the Guru recommends does not come easily without disciplining oneself to have this great attunement with one's own pure or transcendental state. To most people it may turn out to be frustrating should they try to remain in such a state. If a person does not realize his identity to be that of a beginningless and endless existence, which is essentially one of pure consciousness and is so wholly absorbing that nothing is left outside to add to it, to enhance it, or enrich it in any manner, then he should decide that he is in need of help to attune himself to this ideal of equipoise.

This is not a mere ideal, we have before us the examples of great masters like Buddha, Lao Tzu, Christ, Sri Ramakrishna, Narayana Guru or Ramana Maharshi who had all experienced this kind of centralization of consciousness. We should turn to these masters and draw inspiration from their magnificent lives. If they seem to be too far and legendary we should find a living example to relate to.

At no time in the history of the world were such masters totally absent. In our own day we can find humble beings who have perfected their lives by tuning themselves to the greater Self. There is an old saying that the master comes when the disciple is ready. The world at large and the individual have within them a dialectical chance operation that mostly fulfills what the individual looks for. Just as, by sheer chance, a man gets the kind of skill he needs, by some unknown principle, he will also find his master.

To establish bi-polarity with such a blessed one, one should begin the disciplining from a physical level, such as making one's service available to the noble teacher. This will provide us with an opportunity to decipher the meaning of the wakeful world by observing his personal reaction to it. By pondering upon his words of instruction we can decipher the conceptual images of the world of subjectivity. By observing his neutral silence, we can decipher the secret of abolishing incipient memories. From this overall identity with the transcendental we can discover the non-duality of the Transcendence to which we all belong.

Verse 8

oḷimutalām paẓamañ̄cumuntu nāṟum-
naḷikayileṟi nayēna māṟiyāṭum-
kiḷikaleyan̄cumariññu kīẓmaṟikkum-
veḷivuruvēntiyakam viḷaṅṅiṭēṇam.

Enjoying the five fruits, such as beauty,
mounted on a foul-smelling gun and evasively flying back and forth
are five birds; having brought them down, through an inversion,
that radiant inner awareness should fill one's entire being.

Knowledge, awareness, consciousness and the unconscious are inadequate terms referring to the Self. Another expression for the same is the cosmos. The human organism is like a mysterious link between the physical universe and the almost incomprehensible Absolute Being. At the core of each organism there is the experiencing of a consciousness which, like Janus, the double headed Roman god, is facing two opposite directions. One faces the world of objects and the other faces a world of consciousness that sometimes enters into the dark fold of the unconscious and, on rare occasions, allows a penetration into pure transcendence. In the previous verse the ideal possibility of merging with transcendence, after having attained a full comprehension of the secret of the manifestation of the immanent, was given. To most people this is a difficult feat to accomplish.

As an alternative to the achieving of realization by one's own true comprehension, it was suggested that the aspirant can place him or herself in the service of a realized contemplative who is ever awake to the secret of the sacred syllable *aum* — in other words, getting into a bipolar relationship with an absolutist preceptor. It is very difficult to get into a harmonious relationship with a true Guru. One aspect of the Guru belongs to his physical body, his traditional grooming and the personal idiosyncrasies which make him unique. It is both impossible and to a great extent unnecessary and even harmful to get into that stratum of his life. All these embellishments are only like the engravings on a certain container of wisdom, which can be made of something rugged and as worthless as a lump of pig-iron, or exquisitely charming as a very fragile crystal. Many people waste their whole lives either in the difficult task of maintaining beliefs and trusts in a projected value of the worthless alloy of the container, or in infatuation of the crystalline finish of the engraved receptacle.

The other aspect of the Guru is where the "he" or "she" in that person is effaced and the consciousness that animates the Guru's psycho-physical organism is one with the indiscernible and the unnameable where he has no uniqueness. Without undergoing a civic death of the social ego one cannot discover the transcendent ego.

In the present verse, our attention is drawn to the distractions that are offered to the outward-looking face of the socially structured ego. We live in a consumer society where an active campaign to catch the attention of any one or all of our senses is going on all the time. Pain and pleasure are intimately connected with sensory agitations; they are also symmetrically coupled with two other mental states: the sense of gratification and the sense of guilt. One of the major items in the prayers of people belonging to every religion is the invoking of help to avoid temptation. Both the hookers outside and the pleasure seekers inside are adepts in playing vile games of various kinds of cover-up devices of manipulation and ingenious designs of evasion and elusiveness.

Guru compares the pleasure-seeking senses to five birds that are very cunning in the manner in which they gratify their desires. They are depicted as living on the tree of life. We are mortal, and hence the tree on which they rest, hide and enjoy the fruits of their desires is like a snare which can expose them to death at any time.

This verse contains a plethora of metaphors. A student must separate each analogy from the rest to know its full implication. It is a verse for deep reflection. We have seen the analogy of the sense objects as fruits, and of the sense organs as birds. We have seen the analogy of the tree of life as a snare. The Guru also equates the tree to a foul-smelling gun. Like a gun, our body has a hollow in it. The sulfurous smell of the body is well known to everyone, one needs only rub his own skin to get the smell of gun powder. The causes of death stockpiled in our body can defeat any arsenal. Death abolishes all games of life. Another analogy implied in the verse is that of the lotus flower. Its stalk is hollow like the barrel of a gun. The bulb of the lotus is buried in dirt and it lives in stagnant pools. The flower, however, is above water and it opens up to the bright sun. It has attractive petals. The stamen is rich with poller and the flower has honey in it. It is of great attraction to bees, lovers, artists, poets, yogis and, according to the poets, even to the sun. Although its source is something as lowly as dirt its impact on the world is great, yet just a little tap will snap the stalk thus destroying its glory in less than a moment.

All these analogies form only the numerator aspect of the ideogram presented in this verse. At the denominator Guru places the determination of the aspirant as an act of absolute discrimination to act in favour of wisdom. This aspect is analogically alluded to as the vigil of a hunter who can shoot his arrow of discrimination to bring down this sensually monitored mind to its own denominator base. This act of discipline is an uncompromising attitude born of an insight into the true meaning of immanence which implies in it the total value of the Transcendent Being. It is like opening a floodgate into the value vision of the Absolute that will eventually transform every aspect of both the denominator and the numerator with the joy and wonder of the Absolute.

Verse 9

irupuṟavum varumāṟavasthayeppū-
ttoru koṭivannu paṭarnnuyarnnumēvum
taruvinaṭikku tapassuceytu vāẓum-
naranu varā narakam ninaccitēṇam.

Growing on both sides, in a blossoming state,
is the one vine which has come, spread out and risen to the top of
a tree; remember that hell does not come
to the man dwelling in contemplation beneath it.

In spaceless space and timeless time, an amorphous vaporous cloud lay dreaming of some day giving birth to a galaxy. The dream came true. This earth of ours is a tiny speck brought forth from the womb of cosmic manifestation. For several millennia the earth was undecided on what to dream. We can only guess what happened in the cosmic scene when we see a swelling seed about to bring forth a sprout through a crevice of its unbroken shell, and we can only conjecture that the cosmic dream has no beginning and no end. When we sleep, oblivious of everything, there is not even the trace of a dream to betray the potentials lying buried in us that are looking for an opportune moment to burst forth into a Milky Way of a million possibilities. There are no two people in this world who look alike nor, perhaps, even see alike. In spite of our diversities, we can trace the single principle to which we all belong. This is evidenced by the one nebula to which our starry heavens belong, the one earth which is our sweet home, the same principle of the proliferation of life, and the one consciousness veiled with the opacity of the physical sheaths in which it has chosen to glow with several modes of alternations.

What came out of the nebula was not a mere cloud, but endless constellations, solar or similar systems, planets of different magnitude and their moons and satellites. Even a little chip of it, like the earth with its mountains, gorges and ravines, thick forests, plains, desert lands and oceans, is an endless wonder.

An organized crest on the surface of earth called humanity created out of the mud of its mind civilizations of war and peace, built monuments of awe and beauty, sang in exultation and lamented in grief, thus giving to the world the rich legacy of music and poetry. Although man is as insignificant as a worm crawling on its belly, he has always acted as if he were the nerve centre of the cosmos by interpreting for his fellowmen the secret of creation and the moral intent of its creator. Like black holes, dead stars, or extinct vulcanoes, we see on the face of the earth the ruins of great civilizations such as Mohenjodaro and Harappa in Pakistan, the Acropolis in Athens, the Colosseum and the Pompeian ruins in Italy and the ruins of Mayan and Inca temples in South America. Our tree of life stands on the ledge of time with a past history of its dissolution and the future hope of the new potential of manifestation.

No one can deny that there is an all-encompassing existence as the ground for all the passing show of the varieties of transiency we experience here, like the germinating sprout, the unfolding leaves, the budding flowers, the blooming of buds into a feast of colour and fragrance, and ultimately the fruit that brings about the seed to mark the final stage of one unit of emergence. Life is endlessly springing from some unknown depth and after coming to a peak or a crest it falls to pieces. Nothing is lost and nothing is gained.

The cosmic play of the sportive Absolute is compared to a tree which is entirely covered by a creeper that has branched into two and has entwined the tree all over, covering the original form with its own flowers and leaves. The creeper referred to is the world of phenomenality. What is enshrouded by the vine is the numinous. The changeless witness of eternity is analogically referred to as a contemplative sitting in the shade of this tree, passively witnessing both the art and the science of phenomenality. There is a spark of the all-witnessing Self in us as well. Sometimes it alternates with our existential ego. The self-luminous and transcendent witness is fully aware of the changeless reality that appears to be changing into the birth, growth, old age and death of a nebula or a sperm in the biologic stream.

If our personal and existential ego is allowed to merge with the transcendental witness through a process of osmosis, it can also attain the transparency of vision that unveils all the secrets of life. Guru refers to this process as doing *tapas.* The realization that comes through such a vision will save a person from all the snares of the temptation of the phenomenal.

Verse 10

"iruḷil irippavanāru? colka nī" ye-
nnoruvan urappatu kēṭṭu tānumēvam
aṟivatināyavanōṭu "nīyumār" e-
nnaruḷumitin prativākyamēkamākum.

"Who is sitting in the dark? Speak, you!"
In this manner one speaks; having heard this, you also,
to know, ask him, "And who are you?"
To this as well, the response is one.

There is a light in the darkness which becomes all the more bright when one intensifies the darkness outside. This light is the nucleus of one's own consciousness and it gains an identity when it declares itself as "I." It is not a light possessed by anyone, because the possessor and the possession are the same. This pure awareness becomes evident to itself only on the rare occasions when it has nothing else to illuminate or interpret to itself. To pinpoint this experience Guru uses an experimental situation. A man sits in the dark seeing nothing, but he suspects the existence of someone besides himself. Out of sheer curiosity he asks, "Who is sitting in the dark?" In response he hears the reply, "I." The other person also asks, "Who are you, sitting in the dark?" And the first person replies, "I." Do the respective answers of the two people make sense to them?

If we abstract the semantic connotation of the word "I" and do not associate with it any psychological data, such as the quality of the voice, it is not possible to make a mental picture of the other person. To all images associated with people, like their physical stature, mode of dress, colour, racial features, physiognomic distinctions, sex, social position, educational background, moods, etcetera, "I" is the very special answer which makes the questioner's mind boomerang on himself. On hearing the word "I" the questioner becomes fully alive to his own inner awareness when he too says "I." Although he is fully satisfied with the knowledge of another person's existence, which he has discovered by questioning the other, he has not gone beyond the frontiers of the verity of his own existence to decide the existence of another. His recognition of the other is through an act of analogy: he makes an initial *a priori* judgement of the word he heard, "I." The validation of the response is based on the validation of his own existential beingness.

This seemingly simple verse implies the entire secret of the methodology of unitive understanding. The Absolute Being is truth itself and it cannot be known through an act of perception or inference. The only possible introduction of its awareness can come from an *a priori* revelation validated by one who is totally identified with the Absolute Being. For this reason, number one primacy is given in Vedanta to the word testimony, *sabda.*

No articulated word makes any sense unless it corresponds to a concept the listener has in his own mind. The act of listening is in fact a continuous comparison of analogical concepts that the speaker and listener have in their respective minds. The apparent newness of any knowledge emerges from the composition of complementing analogies structured differently than on previous occasion, but no analogy will ever give a total picture.

A systematic rejection of analogies assisted by a nuclear cognition like "I" or "That" can suddenly de-structure the entire scaffolding of the mind so that the pure transcendence of beingness can suddenly emerge into its total assertion. Thus, on the whole, the method of word testimony and analogy is used only to do away with all the crutches of the mind. What results from the cancelling out of a situation and its counterparts, such as the questioner and the respondent, is a total silence which is at once the being and nothingness in an existential appraisal.

Verse 11

"ahamaham" ennaruḷunnatokkeyārā-
yukil akamē palatallatēkamākum;
akalumahantayanēkamākayālī
tukayil aham poruḷum tuṭarnniṭunnu.

"I, I," thus, all that are spoken of,
when carefully considered, inwardly are not many; that is one;
as the receding I-identities are countless
in their totality, the substance of I-consciousness continues.

When I was a child I was too shy to face people and I kept myself mostly indoors or alone among the bushes keeping company with flowers and dragonflies. In my youthful days I had a craze for people and I wanted to talk to multitudes. Now in my middle age I am no longer afraid of people, but I see their collective essence in the depth of my own being and I prefer to sit in silence with my senses turned inward.

Are these three separate "I-s"? They are not. When my intimate friend addresses me, he refers to me as "you" and to himself as "I." When a person who, for some reason, has developed a dislike for me and wants to reproach me points his index finger at me, he wrathfully says "you" and refers to himself as "I." Just as my friend did, I consider his "you" my "I" and my "I" his "you." Are these two "I-s" different? Whether it is that of my friend or my foe, I can understand and appreciate the meaning of "I" only by living it in the essence of what I call "I." Thus, in me there is a sequential variation of "I" that goes on receding from the present to the past. In the same manner, with the plurality of individuation, the extension of "I" is horizontally spread out with several seemingly separate agencies behind each "I."

For a person endowed with a fully co-ordinated comprehension of the vertical and horizontal serialization of the "I" concept there is only one essential "I." It was the "I" that was hushed within me as a lonely child and the "I" that celebrated its youth by gleefully merging with the multitudes. It is the "I" in me and the "I" in you. There is no diversity when the "I" enters into itself and remains in its beingness. If I run around each separate experience and look at the shades and colours of the complexes it brings to the emotional and intellectual texture of the "I" in me and the "I" in you, even that "I" becomes scattered fragments of several conscious units, and the same cannot be different of others when they are treated as separate entities. The wise comprehend it as one.

What is termed here as *ahamporuḷ* is the Self, which by nature is existence, subsistence and the value of all values. All these three aspects come in the experience of the receding ego also as the apprehension of what is existent, the awareness of the mode that is presented in existence and an affectation which directly relates the ego to the value of whatever is presented as an object of awareness. However fragmentary and receding the ego identities are, they are pervaded by the essence of the Self. There can be two possible breaks in the continuation of the self. One is when a person's ego-identity changes from one universe of interest to a totally different universe of interest. This possible chasm is bridged here by saying that the ego is carrying over from one interest to another the same principle of cognition, conation and affection. The second discontinuity comes when the series of ego in a person is terminated by death. That again is no problem, because one man's ego series is only one in countless millions of ego apprehensions and affections. It is only the "I" that disappears, but its essence and momentum continues.

Verse 12

toliyumelumpu malam durantamantaḥ-
kalakaḷumēntumahantayonnu kāṇka!
poliyumitanya poliññu pūrṇṇamākum
valiyorahanta varā varam tarēṇam.

See the skin, bone, dirt and inner urges which end tragically
to which the I-identity is conjoined;
this which perishes is the other; oh, grant the cherished boon
that the great I-identity increases to perfection.

There is nothing like a youthful body of robust health. If it is also complemented by an exuberant mind full of creative ideas and elevating visions of the future, life on earth is a great blessing. Even though some people may enjoy this special grace for 20 or 30 years, the body will eventually start to show signs of age and deterioration. When mankind was marvelling at people like Albert Einstein, Bertrand Russell or Rabindranath Tagore, their ageing and inevitable death caused great anxiety not only to their friends, but also to the whole world. With all the scientific advancements we have made, we have yet to succeed in preserving the youthful spirit and physical existence of even such rare human beings beyond the span of a century.

Consciously or unconsciously we aspire to immortality. Nature's device to immortalize life is the continuation of it through the progeny of its proliferating species. When the main stream of life is taken as a whole, the decay and death of individual bodies can be looked upon as the falling leaves of autumn.

A relative long lease of social life is guaranteed to people of moral and spiritual excellence and to those who contribute to the ennobling of human culture by creating landmarks in the fields of art, literature, science and technology. Of all these varieties of immortalization, none can give solace or satisfaction to an individual who is facing the crucial problems of his own physical health, mental hygiene, moral stamina or spiritual enlightenment. Although our body can look comely and even adorable to a few intimates, it is like a time-bomb with its needle stuck on the zero hour of blast-off. If a person is diabetic, a little scratch on the toe is enough to start a growing catastrophe that could prove fatal.

One of the most scaring experiences is to visit a museum of pathology and see the size of the stones that are extracted from people's gall and urinary bladders, or the tumors taken out of intestines and brains. Why should we nauseate ourselves by even thinking of these horrid things or any other specimen neatly arranged in perfectly labelled bottles? This aspect of life is very sickening. Now, if we took a round through the wards of a mental institution for a change, we would get a glimpse of the ghosts and goblins that hide in our unconscious with their menacing programmes for making life on earth the greatest punishment one can imagine. When we consider these physical and mental disasters, the assurance of a solemn and dignified death looks far more tempting than becoming donors of samples in a pathology museum.

When we look into the lives of certain people with chronic ailments, such as Immanuel Kant, Friedrich Nietzsche and Karl Jaspers, we see what brilliant performances they gave the world in spite of all the physical tortures they had to endure in their daily lives. Other geniuses, like Holderlin, Swinburne, Beethoven and Van Gogh, outlived the traumas of their minds and immortalized their beatific visions. This suggests the existence of a certain personal factor which is capable of rising above physical and mental malfunctions. Edmund Husserl and Karl Jaspers call this the transcendent, which can be in resonance with the Transcendent Being. If that aspect in us can ultimately free itself from the limitations of our embodied state and social entanglements, it will surely become radiant with the effulgence of that one light that illuminates everything. If this personal factor does not become fully purified, it is likely to lead us into the greater evil of becoming pseudo-spiritual monsters who can mislead millions of people into embracing some cult of the most negative or destructive kind.

Considering all these physical disasters, mental aberrations and snares of ego, one can only turn to God with an ardent supplication to be saved from at least one's own fabricated snares.

Verse 13

triguṇamayam tirunīṟaṇiññorīśa-
nnakamalriṭṭu vanaṅṅiyakṣamāṟi
sakalamaẓiññu taṇiññu kēvalattin-
mahimayumaṟṟu mahassilāṇiṭēṇam.

Having offered the flower of your mind to that Lord
smeared with sacred ashes, the three *guṇas*,
having cooled down the senses, unwound everything, and become calm,
when even the glory of aloneness has gone, become established in *mahas*.

We live in a world of ideas, facts and fundamentals. Ideas are vivid when they come and they can be freely structured into patterns and motives if we know how to handle their logical structuring. A fact is rigid, as it is ruled by physical laws and social conventions, but one aspect of it can always be turned against another so as to neutralize its potential or make it aggressively real. The fundamentals imply the real challenge of life and are wrapped in the mysteries of vagueness and uncertainty. These three fields correspond, in a general way, to our thoughts, actions and feelings.

When ideas become structured patterns of thoughts they sit on the surface of the mind as semantic tools and they lose their potential to make a breakthrough from the established concept of our humdrum world. When a genuine idea blazes forth as a leaping flame from the furnace of Absolute Truth, it causes such a conflagration that all relativistic ideas are burned to ashes and the world can no longer be the same for the person to whom this happens. In the transactional world, where actions and reactions are governed by the conventional norms of conformity, life becomes tedious and boredom sits heavily on everybody's conscience as a taskmaster of duty.

When the thrust for soul's freedom erupts as a frenzied volcano, man-made walls of prohibitions and the sceptre of commandments are brushed aside as of little or no relevancy to the vertical unfoldment of the true meaning of life. When the non-essentials, misunderstood and propagated by dull-headed fanatics, form the morbid crust of social mores, there may come from the pen of a grief-stricken poet of unbounded compassion or the tearful eyes of a great lover of mankind a word or even a look that can abolish a whole world of patterns and modes, so that humanity can begin again from scratch and return to the innocence of its childhood with fresh hope and dreams. This tri-basic annihilation of morbid ideas, crude actions and outmoded values are symbolized in this verse by the great God smeared with the ashes of the modalities of nature: *satva, rajas, tamas.*

To understand this perennial source of creation (*mahas*), the boundless source of subsistence and the imperishable value of the ever new theme of fulfillment, one should reconsider one's own ideas, actions and preferences in the light of the Absolute. This can be done only by consciously negating what is taken for granted and by going for reassurance to the very fountain-head of truth. This cannot be done with any sense of leisure, there are no holidays in the quest for the Absolute. Although this might sound like a tall order, what issues from such a discipline is the sundering of all fetters and the simultaneous emergence of a freedom that was never known before.

As our enslaved mind had never before known such freedom, it might become drunk with excitement. A consistent follow-up of the discipline will result in the experience of the same freedom, which will soon become an accomplished fact of the fundamental that governs all ideas, actions and values. There is nothing more to gain than to know that this is possible in this very life itself.

Verse 14

tribhuvana sīma kaṭannu tiṅṅiviṅṅum-
tripuṭi muṭiññu teḷiññiṭunna dīpam
kapaṭayatikku karasthamākuvīle-
nnupaniṣadukti rahasyamōrttiṭēṇam.

Going beyond the boundaries of the three worlds, with all-filling effulgence,
when the three-petaled knowledge has faded out, ever brighter shines that light;
a pretentious seer will never grasp this;
thus, the Upanisads' secret word should be remembered.

A person can look outward and see a world that alternately fascinates and bewilders. He can also look inward and be delighted at the prospect of the possibilities that can be creatively imagined, or be fearful of the negative and depressing phantoms that might haunt his psyche. For many people, living in this world is like being caught between the deep and the devil. This is not the only possibility however. One can also look from the centre of his beingness to a world that has for its substance the same reality of beingness, or he can look into this beingness and see in it the intrinsic worth of the world which he adores.

Both the fool and the wise man live in the same world and are equipped with the same faculties; however, their experience is at great variance with regard to its quality and meaning. The man whose awareness alternates between the changing patterns of the external phenomenon and his internal imagery is bewildered by the great flux which gives him no foothold on which to stand firm, nor any side rail to hold on to. The wise man sees a consistent and constant frame of reference in which even uncertainty comes under the category of the certainty of the law that makes it inevitably uncertain. If the former is assailed by doubts and surprises, the latter foresees eventualities and amuses himself with the wonder that the flux can evoke by corroding into expectations and sometimes nullifying the certitude of a prediction. It is hard for those who are easily deluded to evolve into the fully informed. There are many aspirants for such an elevation, but only a few enter the haven of wisdom.

Conceit is a disease of which man is rarely relieved. We have many accepted classifications and categorizations with which it is easy to separate the sheep from the goats. In the case of sheep and goats the difference is obvious, but when it comes to subtle qualities that characterize personality traits, we are misled by advertised titles. A freshman in a medical school is likely to make himself a physician of renown after several years of intensive training, good discipline and experience. If, however, the possibility is mistaken for an actuality and he offers his services to handle a difficult case which involves risk, he will only be a menace to his patient. Title to wisdom is nowhere different from this. Wishful thinking makes many people identify with unachieved abilities or understanding and this wrong identification becomes their main hurdle to surmount in order to achieve the goal for which they set out on their journey.

The ideal presented in this verse is of a person who is an adept in restraining himself from being misled by the lures of a seemingly fascinating world or from being crippled by its illusory threats. In the same way he is also capable of retaining the valid memory of the rules of transaction so that even when he is fully conversant with the all absorbing beingness of the Transcendent, he can legitimately respond to the natural requirements of the phenomena to which his body and senses belong. He sees the past, the present and the future, what is far off, close by and inside, and the shifting agency of the ego moving back and forth between the roles of the knower, the doer and the enjoyer. True wisdom can transcend all these kinds of triads. Until one gains this rare insight and becomes efficient in living with it, he cannot be called truly wise.

Verse 15

parayuṭe pālu nukarnna bhāgyavanmā-
rkoru paṭināyiramāṇṭoralpanēram;
aṟivapara prakṛtikkadhīnamāyā-
lara noṭiyāyiramāṇṭupōle tōnnum.

To the blessed ones who have sucked the milk of *para*
ten thousand years is but a moment;
but if knowledge succumbs to *apara prakṛti*
half a second seems like a thousand years.

The calendar and the clock play a vital role in the life of many people. Some people carry a diary or an engagement pad filled with their hour to hour and minute to minute programme which runs into several months. It is as if there was a hard taskmaster, a programmer who sits in a corner of our minds dictating what we should do until our limbs are tired and our eyelids become heavy with sleep. For a busy man time passes quickly, but each moment comes to him with such heaviness that he groans under the weight of it. He does not have the problem of killing time, time kills him. There are others for whom time is always on the other side of the great waters. They sit and wait endlessly with nothing to engage their minds or to please their hearts; they are waiting for the realization of a future expectation. For them time drags and their clocks and calendars are slower than slugs.

Physical diseases, social pressures, maladjustments in interpersonal relationships, irrational depressions, unaccountable fears and a host of other troubles weigh on most people so much that only sleep can bring relief to their aching bodies and listless minds. When things are really bad sleep does not come easily, and when it comes it brings such horrid kinds of nightmares that one is afraid of going to sleep. This is what the Guru marks here as the lamentable fate of the one who succumbs to *apara prakṛti. Apara* is that which is not of an absolute order. *Prakṛti* is the fecund nature that goes on replicating and varying modes endlessly.

Even in a person who is always tormented by one disaster or another, sometimes the spark of a joyous moment flickers in his mind; it has no content other than its own brightness. It lingers only for a split second and will only reappear after a long while. Some other people, even when their surface mind attends to various routines and is exposed to the eventualities of day to day living, have within them a calm centre in which the unflickering flame of the consciousness of their beingness is always burning like a temple lamp in the serene atmosphere of its sanctum.

Occasionally, in the course of centuries, there comes one among millions who experiences an all-filling glory of indescribable resplendence that shines both within and without and transforms for him everything he sees and hears into a hymn of praise for the one Absolute, which for him is both the transcendent and the immanent reality of the Self. Guru refers to such a blessed person as one who sucks the milk of *para*. *Para* is that which goes beyond all states of duality. It is the indescribable one arrives at where the duality of the transcendent and the immanent are both cancelled out. It is the state which is no state and the union of existence and knowledge is undifferentiated from *ananda*, which can never be adequately explained. For him who sucks the milk of *para* ten thousand years are as fleeting as a single moment. This is what Plato calls the eternal present. When we have no access to the true light of our own Self, life becomes a big drag.

Verse 16

adhikaviśāla maru pradēśamonnāy
nadi perukunnatupōle vannu nādam
śrutikaḷil vīṇu tuṟakkumakṣiyennum
yatamiyalum yativaryyanāyiṭēṇam.

A very vast wasteland suddenly
flooded by a river in spate—thus comes the sound
that fills the ears and opens the eyes of the one who is never distracted;
such should be the experience of the seer *par excellence.*

A continuous tumult is going on in our mind as several unidentified urges and clashing interests are crying at the top of their voices to catch our attention. In the clang of such confusion it is hard to listen to the silvery voice of the spirit. In his Gitanjali, Tagore makes an earnest appeal to the screeching dwarfs of his ego to hold their tongues so that he might listen to the sweet melody of his Lord. Even the loneliest recluse cannot get away from the procession of loud thoughts that parades through his mind. A sage *par excellence* is he who can silence his inner tumult so that he can become a worthy receptacle to be filled with the elixir of mystical beatitude. The Guru refers to such a sage as the noble among *yatis.*

When life is devoid of its greening fountain of values, the world becomes an arid desert land. In such a situation the scarcity of interest in the external world is more than matched by the unquenchable thirst of the spirit for adorable values. This causes such painful agony to the aspirant that he becomes benumbed and has no sensitivity with which to appreciate the promise of the sublime.

At some zero hour there comes a breakthrough of the impasse caused by the revolt of the sensuousness that wants to feed on the imaginary fodder of the transient. For the blessed one who has silenced the rebellion of his own lower self, the world suddenly becomes so immersed in a flood of delight that every grain of sand on which he treads becomes a pearl of priceless worth.

Verse 17

aẓaleẓumañcitaḷārnnu raṇṭu taṭṭāy
cuẓalumanādi viḷakku tūkkiyātmā
niẓaluruvāyeriyunnu neyyatō, mun-
paẓakiya vāsana, vartti vṛittiyatrē.

Having two tiers of five petals, whence pain arises,
rotating, beginningless, hangs the lamp of the self,
burning as the shadow (of true being), with the oil
of latent urges and mental modifications as the wicks.

Our first experience in life is the irritation of our nervous system, and our first lesson on earth is to formulate out of that irritation patterns of pain and pleasure. Pain-pleasure is a twin experience born of the same stuff which causes agitation of the nervous system. Very early in our life a wedge is driven into that experience so that pleasure becomes acceptable while the pain is to be avoided at all cost.

We never get tired of looking at the petals of a rose, especially when it is illuminated from a favourable angle. In our old age, if cataracts come to deprive us of such pleasures, we think our very soul is sinking into a quagmire of depression. We love light so much. In the summer when the sun is blazing and the sky gives too much glare, we drape our windows with heavy curtains. Similarly when our eyes become sensitive, due to some disease, we protect them with dark glasses. Our eyes are such neatly made devices that we can effortlessly drop our eyelids when we do not want to see something. Compared to our eyes, our ears are at a great disadvantage. We would plug them permanently if we were to listen only to the screeching traffic of our noise polluted cities. There are other tickling treats, however, for our ears: a beautiful symphony for instance, or the whispering of a beloved person telling us something that our soul craves to hear. The main traffic between two souls passes through their organs of hearing. In a metaphorical sense we can say that all our five senses have their own favourite kinds of light. They are pleasurable only at a certain pitch. When the input is below that pitch we complain of inadequacy and when the stimulation climbs above that pitch it becomes acutely painful. Thus, our doors of perception can give us a choice of either heaven or hell.

What is it that pleases us when we look at a rose? We never even give a thought to the light that comes reflected from that rose. The stimulation that particular light causes to our supersensitive optic nerve has a certain quality of agitation. This agitation comes between two real entities. On one side is the knowing consciousness; its pure state is mutilated and modified by the nervous stimulation. On the other side is the pure light that travels from one object to another; the energy of light is made part of a relay race. Some indescribable quality of the flower, which altered the frequency of the light that fell on it, brings the message of the flower by way of the reflected rays that are delivered to the retina. At this point, the message is decoded and deciphered into a totally different language, that of a nerve impulse instead of sunlight. The light of the soul and the light of earth coming from opposite sides are now fused into one single entity called the visual experience. Thus, in every experience of pain as well as pleasure we are forfeiting our right to know what is inside and what is outside.

Without hesitation we call a shadow the light. All the five senses are thus manufacturing for us countless patterns of shadows with which to structure a perceptual world. We even transform ourselves into a perceptually and conceptually structured shadow. It is no wonder that Plato caricatured our life on earth as shadows living a shadowy life in the dark cellar of a cave.

We presume that there is an external world constituted of five basic elements: the earth which smells, water which has taste, fire which reveals forms, air which gives the experience of touch and the ether which produces sound. We also presume that there is a person in us who can smell, taste, see, touch and hear. Who is that person? No one knows. And what is that world? No one knows. The two put together make perfect counterparts of deception. It is like an imaginary lamp of two tiers, one representing the physical and the other the psychic. The wicks are the five senses, the oil that burns is the incipient memory of this mythical being called the individuated self, and the flames are the painful agitations that are accepted as pleasure, much the same way as the thorns of the cactus are appreciated by camels as the delicacy of the desert.

Verse 18

ahamirulallirulākil andharāy nā-
mahamahamennariyātirunnitēṇam;
arivatināl ahamandhakāramalle-
nnarivatininnaneyārkkumōtitēṇam.

The "I" is not dark; if it were dark we would be in a state of blindness,
unable to know even "I, I";
as we do know, the "I" is not darkness;
thus, for making this known, this should be told to anyone.

There are moments of deep despair and darkness in our lives, yet even on such occasions the consciousness of "I" continues to shine as pure awareness; only what it is aware of is darkness. Even when the most intense physical darkness blinds our eyes, we do not lose sight of this inner awareness. It is true that people vary as regards the amount of information they have about things. We can also see that there is a difference in the quality of their comprehension a wise man can be differentiated from a dull-minded person. In spite of all these differences, the mind of every person is animated by his own light within. So if a person says, "I am ignorant," it is to be taken only in a relative sense.

In the *Kena Upaniṣad* (II.2.) it is said: "It is known to him to whom it is unknown; he does not know to whom It is known. It is unknown to those who know well, and known to those who do not know." Thus, according to the seers of the Upaniṣads, recognition of one's ignorance is considered the first step of one's pilgrimage to wisdom. First of all, to say "I do not know," there should be a light of consciousness to know what is not known. Secondly, there should be the discriminating function of consciousness, which alone can decide what is known and what is not known. If these inner faculties operate soundly, then one only needs to direct that consciousness toward its own ultimate realization. Thus, potentially, every person has a right to know and to realize.

In our social circles we recognize certain people as sages, seers or knowledgeable ones. This brings to one's mind the doubt that he is probably of an inferior nature and he does not have the capacity to know. Guru in this verse makes the appeal that such fear should be removed from everybody's mind, so that all can confidently move into the direction of right knowledge.

According to Buddhist legend, when Gautama became awakened as the Buddha, he marvelled at the truth that became known to him and he thought it was too much for an ordinary person to comprehend so he decided to keep his realization a secret. At this point Brahma Sampati appeared before him and said, "Oh Blessed One, you have become the Buddha, the Awakened One. What you have come to know can save the whole world; do not hold onto it as a secret. The world is sleeping and only a thin layer of darkness veils their eyes from right comprehension. If you share your noble truth, many will rise from their stupor to accept it." This admonishing was taken seriously by the Buddha and he wandered far and wide around India for over 50 years to awaken people to their own inner light.

When people believe they are ignorant, this negative knowledge brings with it both depression and inertia. They lose the capacity to seek, to strive and to understand. Thus, when they perpetuate their ignorance, life becomes truly dreadful and pathetic. Although we are not of the same stature as the Buddha or the Christ, in our own simple way we can share the little joys of our lives and bring at least a few people to their own centre so that they can realize the worthwhileness of their own lives.

Verse 19

aṭi muṭiyaṟṟamatunṭituṇṭatuṇṭe-
nnaṭiyiṭumādima sattayuḷḷatellām;
jaḍamity sarvamanityamām; jalattin-
vaṭivine vittu taraṅgamanyamāmō?

The bottom, the top, the end, that is real, this is, no, that is – in this way people quarrel; the one primal reality is all that is;
all this inertial matter is transient;
except as a form of water could a wave ever arise?

It is hard for most of us to remember what happened yesterday. Our own childhood has become a half-forgotten legend, yet we are curious to know when the universe began and how it was when it began. Some people believe in an old God who created this world to kill his boredom. Others, being more clever, came to the conclusion, after a few centuries of probes and calculations, that it all began with a big bang. A big bang of what? Of course no one knows.

What you and I know for sure is that we live in a world of flux. The author of the *Bhagavad Gita* confesses his ignorance of the beginning and the end of this world. He agrees with us in the fact that he knows only the middle part. We have enough problems of our own without bothering about either the first cause or the final end. Even our personal issues are sometimes so complicated that we cannot make head or tail of them and we decide to take a bold stand only because of the pressure of the circumstances.

It is only natural that my food is your poison, so there is every possibility that you will challenge my stand and offer an alternative. Much of the change of flux in the society is caused by the lack of agreement among its members. However, there is an unconscious faith in us that the truth is always one. Similarly, we must at least expect that there should be a general agreement in our conception of higher values, such as beauty, goodness and justice, otherwise people would not have joined hands as one single force to bring about the French Revolution on hearing the slogan "Equality, liberty and fraternity". It is true that the votaries of this slogan did not live the spirit of it for long, but that does not prove that the oneness of human values is not a true principle.

There is an existential prayer which throws light on the agreement and disagreement, hope, the frustration of mankind:

I do my thing, and you do your thing.
I am not in this world to live up to your expectations
and you are not in this world to live up to mine.
You are you and I am I.
And if by chance we find each other, it's beautiful
If not, it can't be helped.

Our world has a history of blast and counter-blast of agreements and differences, but whether we agree or not, some great force is continuously and consistently bringing about day and night, puts us to sleep and wakes us up. We are stimulated to eat, mate and keep the zest for life burning within us even when we see nothing but destruction all around us.

The great philosopher Sankara said, "Only the cause is real and not the effect." According to him, the cause is without qualities and, being undifferentiated, cannot be a thesis for intelligent consideration. Thus, he gives us an exposition of the basis or ground of truth. This position is challenged by Ramanuja who extols the magnificence of the effect.

Consider a small seed and the mammoth tree that comes from it; its branches spread out in all directions covered by green foliage and overladen with flowers of colourful petals and sweet fragrance. If you wait a while, you might even gather its edible fruits. So what comes from the top cannot be judged by merely looking at the base.

It is into this world of conflicts that we have come. In this context Narayana Guru emerges as the peace maker, he agrees with the partial truth of everybody's argument. He points out that the ocean has a surface and a depth. On the surface there is room for all kinds of changes, such as high tide and low tide, silence, stillness, gentle ripples, rolling waves or mountain-like surging tidal waves. In its depth, hidden away from the surface, the ocean conceals several kinds of aquatic beings, minerals, oils and treasures like pearls. The navigating on the surface and the vertical submergence into the ocean's depth give different kinds of experiences. A wise person should have a unitive way of recognizing all these facts. Such a vision will help us to be reconciled with the inevitable differences that are bound to be expressed by people who look at truth from different vantage points. This knowledge brings peace and tolerance into our lives. It gives us a sober mind to agree with and it encourages us to cooperate with all.

Verse 20

ulakinu vēṟoru sattayillatuṇṭe-
nnulakar urappatu sarvamūhahinam;
jaḷanu vilēśayamennu tōnniyālum
nalamiyalum malarmāla nāgamāmō?

Other than this the world has no reality;
"there is" – all such that people say is without reflection;
even if to a numbskull it appears to be a snake,
will a fresh flower garland ever become a serpent?

Many people think that a spiritual life is not this life. It must be something very different in order to be spiritual. Many cherished things should be given up and one should get into a whole new routine and discipline. The dichotomy between spiritual life and worldly life is a prejudice perpetuated by religion. There is only one thing here, and that is this world and our funny, crazy or wonderful minds to experience it with. Everything we see outside opens a window to experience what is inside. For instance, in the froth of a coffee cup we can see Joan of Arc furiously charging her steed in battle. Actually it is only a smudge of cream sticking to the side of the glass. Although we have never experienced Joan of Arc fighting like hell in the battlefield, our love for heroism must have created such and similar images at an impressionable age which then come back as vivid memories. In our creative power we excel the creator of the factual world by posting on his creation a million other imaginations of our own which have no basis other than our fancy.

In our meditation on verse 17, we have already come to know how easily we substitute shadow for light. We have also seen that the verity of existence and the confirmation of values are directly related to the existence of the Self and its innate quality of being the ground of all values. As our life here is a blend of light and darkness, knowledge and ignorance and consequently also pain and pleasure, when a person to whom this world is an arid desert-land of no meaning or beauty wakes up in his Self, every grain of sand will turn into a pearl of priceless worth.

There is nowhere to go from here. Don't fancy that there is some other world. Right where you are, you can create one hundred other worlds if you like. They can be delightful or dreadful to suit your state of mind. If a man has a large treasure he will delightedly estimate its worth, but the fear of burglars shooting him and running off with his treasure will also make him shudder. Thus, the same value can also make our mind go in two entirely different tangents: one ruminating on the possibility of a prosperous life and the other worrying about an imminent disaster. When a person is in the fondest embrace of his or her much longed for beloved, out of nowhere a sudden fear or doubt can creep into the lover's mind suggesting the possibility of a rival luring the beloved away, and the very peak of happiness can become a schizophrenic disaster.

All such troubles in life arise from the Self playing hide and seek with our mind. When a man, tired after his day's work, hurriedly goes to his unlit room and settles down on his bed, should he happen to touch something moist and cool he may start with sudden fear on looking at the object he touched if he sees it as a reptile-like thing covered by dark and bright spots; he may even give out a primal scream. Later, when he realizes that it is a garland of the finest flowers picked and strung by his beloved and sprinkled with rose water, he will return to it feeling highly honoured and will wear it around his neck.

To a wise man this world is such a garland strung with the finest values man can conceive, but he needs to gain a transparency of vision which can see, through all these variegated names and forms, the wonder of the one Self that is of pure existence, subsistence and value.

Verse 21

priyamoru jātiyitenpriyam tvadīya-
priyamapara priyamennanēkamāyi
priyaviṣayam prati vanniṭum bhramam; tan-
priyamapara priyamennaṟiññiṭēṇam.

Endearment is one kind; this is dear to me
your preference is for something else;
thus, many objects of endearment are differentiated and confusion comes;
what is dear to you is dear to another also; this should be known.

Being is one thing and seeing is another. Seeing is a partial experience, it neither highlights a concept, nor synchronizes a concept with a percept. Even to the wisest of men a rat is a rat and a cat is a cat. However, through an absolute empathy, a person can transcend the conditional limitations of name and form; in fact, this transcendence vouchsafes the transmutation of names and forms, and everything will remain the same to him even after achieving perfect transcendance. Now the difference in experience is not in belonging to his act of perception or conception, but in his being one with the existential unity of everything and in the holistic appreciation of the unity of everything substantiated by unbroken consciousness. The worth of each in itself becomes, as it were, the reflection of the oné sun in several mirrors.

The kind of programming and conditioning to which we are exposed in our everyday life is such that sooner or later we become alienated from our beingness and we become identified with very many personal likes and dislikes, individual things and conceptual ideas. Recognition of dear values in a thing, a person, or an ideology alienated from total beingness is like a bee in the bonnet which cannot be shared universally with all.

When two people have their separate likes and dislikes, a clash or a conflict of interest arises between them. When the same people find their union at a deeper level, such as in their beingness, their conceptual identities undergo a radical transformation so that their knowledge can be in tune with their beingness. For instance, when a person loves another person intensely, even though the other person's habits and preferences are contrary to his likes and dislikes, the sheer love for the other acts like an alchemy; it blends their lives in such a way that both of them come to appreciate the same values. This is not happening from above by making rational programmes of unifying their interest, but it happens almost unconsciously from beneath, as it were.

The discovery of the full worth of one's life is accomplished by returning to the one beingness to which everything and everyone alike belongs. In this rediscovery, one learns to appreciate that his happiness is implied in the happiness of all, and the happiness of others are as much of his concern as his own happiness.

Verse 22

priyamaparanteyatenpriyam; svakīya-
priyamaparapriyamiprakāramākum
nayamatināle narannu nanma nalkum-
kriyayaparapriya hētuvāyvarēṇam.

The happiness of another – that is my happiness;
one's own joy is another's joy. – this is the guiding principle;
that action which is good for one person
should bring happiness to another.

From the wriggling worm in a ditch to the philosopher in meditation, all are seeking happiness. Every movement of the body and pulsation of the mind is in search of happiness. Most people think that happiness comes by pampering the senses or pleasing the mind. Our senses do not know what is painful or pleasurable. A sensation becomes painful or pleasurable only when the sense organs are in contact with the mind.

What is it that pleases the mind? Two factors gladden our minds, one is explicit and the other is somewhat concealed from our gross perspective. Let us first consider the explicit cause. In our mind there are many latent urges and unconscious desires which seek gratification. When we place ourselves in an environment and then move from that environment to another, opportunities arise for one desire or another to relate itself to an external factor in which the possibility of its gratification is visualized. An effort is then made to exploit that situation so as to derive gratification. If the attempt succeeds it brings pleasure and if it fails it brings frustration. In addition to desires, there are also hidden fears of pain-giving situations. Some of the moves we make are to avoid such situations. If we are successful, we experience a sense of security and consequent happiness.

All instances of search for pleasure and gratification of desire involve us in some action. We can in fact say that all actions are motivated by the desire for happiness. When we are in pursuit of pleasure we seem to think that the object of pleasure has the ability to produce pleasure in us. Mostly we are infatuated with that expectation. If we only knew that happiness is a state of mind and it has come from within us, we would not be so rash in making our pursuit blind and aggressive.

Now let us consider this subtle and concealed cause of happiness. The true nature of our Self is its self-founded existence in pure consciousness. It is free of all kinds of miseries and is at peace with itself. A mind that is running after sense objects thinks of the Self as an unknown alien entity which is difficult to know and realize. Although mind has no light of its own other than what is derived from the Self, with the aid of the senses it converts, like a kaleidoscope, the light of the Self into many structured patterns of a fragmentary character.

The natural law of homogeneity fuses existence with existence, knowledge with knowledge and happiness with happiness. When two people come together without effort, they recognize each other's existence. They do not hinder the free flow of their consciousness with private motivations and their knowledge easily mingles as they take to each other with great ease. Without any apparent reason this sense of belongingness brings peace and happiness. Separative notions such as "I" and "you" disappear from their minds and they think of themselves as two persons bracketed into one. Thereafter they spontaneously refer to themselves using words like "us," "ours" and "we." Here a person that was at first apprehended as the other has been transformed into non-other. This kind of togetherness is experienced between lovers, husbands and wives, parents and children and between dear friends. This effortless union is effected by the natural happiness of the Self and by effecting the apparent duality that is caused by physical conditions.

When the outward zest for pleasure and its source is seen more and more within the Self, ego boundaries become effaced and compassion flows more easily in all directions. Such an attitude makes life joyous as we find the union of everybody's happiness through continuous acts of sharing.

Verse 23

aparanu vēṇṭiyaharnniśam prayatnam
kṛpaṇata viṭṭu kṛpālu ceytiṭunnu;
kṛpaṇan adhōmukhanāy kiṭannu ceyyu-
nnapajaya karmmamavannuvēṇṭi mātram.

For the sake of another, day and night performing action,
having given up self-centred interests, the compassionate person acts;
the self-centred man is wholly immersed in necessity,
performing unsuccessful actions for himself alone.

No one in this world is an isolated entity. Our abilities, commitments and responsibilities are to be shared with at least a few people. No one can totally abstain from action. Just to keep the body going one has to breathe, eat and keep the body and the environment clean. All these come under the category of daily imperative actions. Apart from this, there are actions that need to be performed because of our commitment to society, such as the pursuance of one's vocation, for instance. The third kind are optional actions and we may perform them only if we choose; these are incidental actions.

A responsible doctor cannot suddenly decide to treat the casualties on his hands lightly. Parents cannot shirk their responsibilities when their children are too young to take care of themselves. These are examples of imperative actions. Jesus' example of the Good Samaritan illustrates an incidental action.

Of the three kinds of actions enumerated, incidental action implies a deeper spiritual significance than that of imperative and daily actions. Our commitment is born of free choice and that choice is motivated by a unitive understanding that recognizes our identity with the Self in others as well. A father or mother, duty bound to their child, are under social duress. We can say that social mores are based on the fraternity of all beings, but it can also be interpreted in terms of convenience as theorized by Hobbes, Bentham and Machiavelli. Our life flows between the banks of compassion and selfishness. Nature pushes us toward the bank of selfishness when our personal identity is threatened. Our spiritual belongingness attracts us to the opposite bank of compassion when others exposed to danger require our services.

A person with a strong and healthy spiritual identity places his own self as one among others and thus acts out of compassion even when his own self-preservation is at stake. Compassion is the most dominant note of a cluster of values such as love, rejoicement, peace, justice, freedom and fraternity. The realization of all these values is experienced as different degrees of happiness. Even the sharing of pain or grief can have in it an element of spiritual happiness when it is of an altruistic order. Actions motivated by pure selfish need are of the pain/pleasure complex and are of little worth.

People who are obsessed with the idea of "I," "me" and "mine" are blinded by their ego and they hardly notice the inflow of compassion from others. They build around themselves strong walls of separation and they decline responsibilities. As there is no trust in others, they become calculating and carry with them many secrets which increase their paranoia. Their lives are filled with intrigues and manipulations. Such people give way to despair and become heavy on those who are willing to show them compassion. From one disillusionment they go to a new fantasy, only to be once again disillusioned and thrown into the ditch of frustration. These unfortunate people always see long dark shadows of failure obstructing their path in every attempt they make to find an avenue to success.

When compassion dawns in the firmament of our life as our guiding star we become easily acceptable to others and we also detect in everyone something good to love and accept. Encouraged by the showing of love and happiness we may even become strong enough to commit ourselves with unlimited liability. The world will always find a good friend in a kindly person who is not daunted by reproaches and reprovals. Such a pleasant person brings out his or her goodness spontaneously. The sun shines and does not radiate darkness because it is its nature to shine, and so only good comes to the world from the compassionate sage as he engages in action without feeling that he is doing anything.

Verse 24

avan ivan ennariyunnatokkeyōrttā-
lavaniyil ādimamāy orātmarūpam;
avan avan ātma sukhattināca rikku-
nnavayaparannu sukhattināy vareṇam

"That man," "this man" – thus, all that is known
in this world, if contemplated, is the being of the one primordial self;
what each performs for the happiness of the self
should be conducive to the happiness of another.

What is the purpose of my life? This is a question which many people want to answer for themselves. To eat and drink, to mate and multiply are the common lot of all living beings and on this count man is not different from all other animals.

What makes man human? Man is the only animal who counts and calculates, writes poetry, fabricates a language with several thousand different intonations with which to express his ideas and who builds schools and universities and takes pride in founding national libraries. The realization of a purpose is discerned by looking at the nuclear value of its motivation. The purpose of this pen is to write, if it fails it is no longer a pen and it can be thrown away. The central value of man is that he is capable of knowing and sharing his knowledge with his fellow man. In essence, he is knowledge.

Knowledge and self are not two. The operational efficiency of knowledge is evident when a person says "yes" or "no." To say "yes," one should know what truth is and how what is presented conforms to the requirements of truth. The word "no" proclaims dissent. Without a normative notion, genuine or defective, one cannot agree or disagree. Truth determines everything.

The truth that governs the knowledge of man is not something private or personal, it is the one principle that covers everything. The basic element of the material world is hydrogen. A hydrogen atom is structured with one electron and one proton. There is determination in it, it does not vary. That uniformity can be seen in the structuring of the atoms of all elements. Even when the atom of one element combines with the atom of another, its basic structure does not change. For example, water, which is made up of hydrogen and oxygen, does not show the qualities of either hydrogen or oxygen, but the atomic structure continues to be unchanged even when combined into the molecules of water.

From the hydrogen atom to the monkey, we see that the evolutionary process in nature is governed by certain natural laws that are universal and predictable. These laws decide all the functional properties of organic and inorganic bodies. These laws are not revealed to lower forms of life. Man is the consciousness of nature. It is as if nature, in its entirety, has within it an insight that easily merges with the faculty of human reasoning. When man introspects and goes to the very source of the truth that enunciated all the laws of the universe, he does not think that he is a stranger in this world. The labyrinth of the inner secret of the universe is like a parental home for him. He claims knowledge of it as if he has a right to know what he has inherited, and nature hands over to him the keys of one secret after another as he proves himself worthy of receiving those truths.

Thus, when man finally establishes himself as the immortal indweller of the cosmos and the custodian of his knowledge, he does not see anything as alien. In such a state he is not one embodied person looking upon another as a stranger, he is the self of all and he recognizes it.

The nature of the self is a transparency of its awareness and the freedom from the aches and pains of ignorance. To a person who has realized this truth, the suffering of another person is a blemish in universal consciousness. He recognizes his unlimited liability to cleanse the world consciousness of its smudges of impurity. This commitment to perpetuate universal goodness makes compassion the central motivating force in his life.

When an artist or a musician of exceptional ability loses the capacity to express his talent because of old age, we continue to honour him as a musician or an artist. Such kind of favouritism is never shown, however, to a good man. A good man must always be good, his past virtue will not give him licence to show caprice afterwards. A person's realization does not confer upon him any lifelong guarantee of wisdom. The transparency of his vision of universal oneness and goodness should prevail as a fact of life to the very last moment of his life. For this reason a realized person is always dedicated to the welfare of all sentient beings and is a responsible custodian of truth.

Verse 25

oruvanu nallatum anyanallalum cē-
rpparu toẓil ātmavirōdhiyōrttiṭēṇam;
paranu param paritapam ēkitunnō-
reri narakābdhiyil vīṇeriññiṭunnu.

What is good for one person and brings misery to another
such actions are opposed to the self, remember!
those who give great grief to another
will fall into the fiery sea of hell and burn.

We live in a beautiful world. Every morning the sun rises in the east like a golden disk. From the ocean to the mountain and from the mountain to the ocean soothing winds blow. Mother Earth is never tired of producing crop after crop. At home and in the neighbourhood we have people to love. Talented artists, poets, musicians and actors reveal many shades of beauty to give us endless inspiration. Saviours, prophets, wise men and philosophers have enriched the heritage of man with their wisdom. Among us there are many dedicated workers who are trying to make this world a lovable place. In spite of all this, life on earth is not considered a very happy experience. Jesus referred to it as a world of crosses. Buddha saw nothing but pain. In the Gita, Kṛṣṇa speaks of the world as the abode of sorrow. In ancient myths and legends we read of hell-fires and purgatories. When America dropped atom bombs on Hiroshima and Nagasaki, what we saw was not a mythical hell, but, to our horror, a literally burning fire. Only recently the demons of science invented the neutron bomb. America, the USSR, China, France and England have stockpiles of deadly nuclear weapons which could end life on earth. Fear dominates the lives of people holding reins of power. National schizophrenia has become a universal menace.

It is in such a world that an individual has to care for his happiness and be responsible to his brother as a loving neighbour. The self of man is not a private spark embedded in the human skull. It is the one existential truth that permeates everything, including what appears to be lifeless and inert. It is the intelligence implied both in the structure and function of things. The harmony of its laws is experienced as beauty, peace and love. Realization is the experiencing of one's own unity with the all-embracing Word. That is why in the *Bhagavad Gita,* Kṛṣṇa asks Arjuna to raise the self by the self and never to let his own self down. In Plato's dialogue, *Charmides,* Socrates proves that the self is the source of both goodness and evil. According to St. Augustine the desertion of onself from God and the loss of the power to see goodness and beauty are the characteristics of evil.

When we grab what rightfully belongs to another, we think it is unimportant. We try to forget our evil deeds, but in spite of all our rationalizations we experience the prick of our conscience. Accumulated feelings of guilt make the mind smoky and ultimately cause such opacity that the mind becomes too benumbed to appreciate any value. This can be called the cancer of the soul. A pinprick in any part of the body makes the whole body shiver with pain; like that, the pain and darkness of the venom of an individual's negativity can spread through the whole social body. The very first step one can take to redress the world of its misery is to make one's own life righteous.

Verse 26

avayavamokkeyamarttiyāṇiyāy ni-
nnavayaviyāviyeyavariccitunnu;
avan ivan ennatināl avan ninaykku-
nnavaśatayāmavivēkamonninālē.

Holding the limbs together, remaining like a bolt,
the limb owner envelops as vaporous being;
for this reason, "that man" and "this man" arise in this way—
so that man believes, due solely to the weakness of non-discrimination.

Among human beings there are no two people exactly alike in body, mind or personality traits. The fingerprint is considered to be unique. The formation of the skin on the pad of the thumb is considered by criminologists to be very important for the identification of a person who tries to conceal his true identity behind a mask. Fingerprints, however, won't help reveal one's true beingness, for that we need a unifying principle, not a differentiating one.

Look at the bodies of gymnasts or boxing champions, their muscles are like steel. If, for some reason, they choke and fail to breathe for four or five minutes, their bodies will crash to the ground with irreversible consequences. Should the breath leave the body completely, it will first stiffen, then inflame and finally fall apart. The skeletal system, the muscles, all the bodily functions, the sensory and motor systems, memory, reasoning, the will to act and action all depend on the autonomous function of breathing.

The first function we performed on coming out of our mother's womb was to breathe, thereafter we do not stop till death claims our last breath. Nobody knows who has the agency of keeping the respiration going. We may say it is the living principle in us; but what is that? And when and how did it originate? According to biologists or natural scientists, the life that pulsates in us has flowed continuously through many structured organisms over millions of years. The rules of our life not only go beyond the human race, but they have a unified origin even in the kind of stuff that has evolved into the present solar system. This elusive principle called life, which keeps our hearts pulsating rhythmically and makes our lungs expand and contract, has performed the same functions millions of times before in organisms of varying shapes and states of consciousness.

A search for this principle will reveal not only a kinship with the people of our neighbourhood or humanity at large, but will also take us beyond the pale of vegetative life to consider salts and minerals as our next of kin as well. When our universal relationship with the rest of the world is such, how shameful it is for us to live only within the confines of the selfish interest of one embodied person.

Although we carry this body around as our most intimate instrument from the day of birth, our understanding of it is shamefully meagre. Even a ninety-year old person can remember his childhood days with great clarity. Who is keeping all the impressions of life intact in the mythical engrams of the so-called "black box" of the mind? And who supplies those memories to consciousness, without even one second of delay, when there is a need to recall them? Pondering on the mysteries of life will only bring us to even less familiar regions and will close us to the secrets that would make us stand in awe and bewilderment. Even after knowing everything one is still compelled to ask, "What is all this?"

The confusion that ensues from the plurality of chaotic configurations causes distrust and fear of even the nearest of kith and kin. Peace and joy come when one sees the boundless extension of one's life flowing in all directions and mirrored, or even sometimes sculptured, in the life of others.

Verse 27

iruḷil irunnaṟiyunnatākumātmā-
vaṟivatu tānatha nāma rūpamāyum
karaṇamotindriya karttṛ karmmamāyum
varuvatu kāṇka mahēndra jālam ellām

Sitting in the dark, that which knows is the self;
what is known then assumes name and form,
with the psychic dynamism, senses, agency of action and also action;
see how it all comes as *mahēndra* magic!

This world can be compared to a great magical performance in which the magician produces things out of nothing and makes his audience feel wonder-struck. He creates hilarious situations that make people laugh and he conjures hideous sights that make them tremble with fear. He angers them by making them feel deceived,then he evokes a sense of pity in them and he finally satisfies them with his tricks. His audience cannot decide where to draw the line between the truth and falsehood of his show. Life is also a grand show like this. Our senses cannot discern the truth of what they perceive and the magician behind the senses is the mind. The senses are called *indriya* and the ruler or mind is called *Mahēndra,* the Lord of the Senses. In this verse Guru describes the world as the magic of *Mahēndra.*

A sleeping man has no ego. He does not love or hate, nor does he feel any obligations. When he wakes up his sense of duty also wakes and he experiences a certain compulsion to engage in one activity after another. He is proud of some of his actions and ashamed of some other activities. He has moments of inspiration and of frustration. It is as if a panel of directors is behind his mind. One voice goads him to act and another sits in judgement telling him that this is good and that is bad, this should be done and that should not be done. Another conspiring voice says, "There is a loophole. You can make this acceptable by doing it a different way." Still another voice is amused by the jollities of life and occasionally its laughter can be heard. There is also a hysterical voice which, again and again, interrupts all activities and laments in self-pity. The handmaids of all these voices are memories of different shades of vividness.

The whole show is kept going by a procession of interrogations coming one after another: "What is next?" "What do you mean?" "How can it be?" "Which?" "When?" "Who?" "Where?" "What?" and so on. No one knows who is supposed to answer all these questions, the same mind must labor to find the answers.

Although there is no break in the stream of consciousness, interests create temporal domains of their own dominance. Both the fulfilled and the frustrated interests are relegated to the past. What is at hand is considered all-important and it is of the present. Future possibilities may cause slight anxiety and a sense of urgency pushes away what is currently engaging the mind. Mind has its own spatial arrangements in which to structure its thought clusters, value materials and the correlation of associated memories.

What a complex thing is the consciousness that animates each individual being! A general veil of ignorance obstructs one's sight from having a total vision of the whole complex of consciousness. Behind the veil is the self that is grounded on itself and is illuminated by its own light. The veiling shadows and the negative principle exist only in relation to the light of the self. The self is independent and the phenomenon of its experience is dependent. That which remains concealed in darkness shines by its own light and reveals everything that should be known as the self of all.

All the Upaniṣads explain the nature of the Self, yet none give a precise definition of the Self as this verse– "Sitting in the dark, that which knows is the Self." In other words, the Self is that which shines without the agency of a second, and also knows of its illumination and what is illuminated.

Verse 28

aṭi muṭiyaṯṯaṭi toṭṭu mauliyantam
sphuṭamaṟiyunnatu turyya bōdhamākum;
jaḍamaṟivīlatu cinta ceytu collu-
nniṭayil irunnaṟivallaṟiññiṭēṇam.

Without bottom or top, from the bottom to the crest where it terminates–
what is known vividly is *turīya* consciousness;
inert matter does not know; having understood this,
know that what is said to remain in between is not knowledge.

Everybody has some knowledge of something. Mostly the knowledge we speak of is information of things, people, events and interrelations of properties. Now and then we come to a point where it is natural for us to say, "I do not know." In a previous verse the Guru defined the self as the knowledge which shines by its own light in an otherwise all-enveloping darkness. What is the darkness he speaks of? Is it the ignorance we are recurrently confronted with? The recognition of ignorance itself is an act of knowledge. When a person says, "I do not know," it implies two factors. One is the experience of a void, an impasse, a psychological block and the sense of helplessness, and the other is the dissatisfaction of not having experienced a postulated or hypothesized knowledge.

A well-known discipline with which to seek and find knowledge is science. In spite of the enthusiastic pursuit of many truthful seekers in this field, those who have mastered it, like Einstein, Max Plank, Rutherford, Heisenberg, Schrodinger, Sir Arthur Eddington and Bertrand Russell, have stepped down from the claim of absolute knowledge to a modest and humble stand, then told the world not to expect from the scientist a final answer to any ultimate question. All they can assure us of is a statistical approximation of what each observer finds from a particular angle of vision, which, in all probability, must be coloured with the state of mind of the observer. Even though the basic teachings of the *rsis* of the Upanisads, the Chinese sages, the Buddha and Christ are looked upon as the echoes of perennial truth, there is a need to follow up the latest revisions in the field of science, so as to keep oneself acquainted with the natural laws that are newly discovered and the earlier findings which have proved either incorrect or inadequate.

What makes it so difficult to have absolute knowledge of things? Nature, to which our mind and body also belong, has in it inertia as one of its main qualities. It is no wonder that our mind is subjected to a blockage caused by its own inertia. The claims of tangibility and verifiability by direct perception have two major disadvantages. Almost all perceptual experiences are lived within the frame of reference of our dreams, without having to use the external organs of sense. The so-called immediacy need not be attributed only to the wakeful moments of perception; the certitude from whthin, during the dream, is as strong and clear as we perceive it in the wakeful state. If the wakeful state sublates the validity of the dream state, the dream state also sublates the experience of the wakeful. Secondly, the universality of the sense data is arrived at by the common consent of what is otherwise confined to each person's private experience.

The darkness which the Guru speaks of covers the state of the wakeful, the dream and deep sleep. The experiences of these three states come under the category of the gross, the subtle and the causal. The Self mentioned in the previous verse is the impassionate witness of all these states and it is mentioned in the *Maṇḍukya Upaniṣad* as the fourth state, *turīya.* Non-cognition of duality is the mark of *turīya.* No amount of information makes that knowledge better or worse and it is never more clear or less clear. It is not relativistic, it is the Absolute.

The knower of the self calls knowledge only that which is non-differentiated, although, within it there is the negative sphere which accounts for all differentiations. When we look at the self this way, we can say that the world-consciousness is the darkness which resides within the consciousness of the self and operates as the proliferation and actualization of all incipient memories. It is like a dark shadow caused by a bright light; it should not be treated as knowledge.

All that fills the pages of voluminous encyclopedias is to be considered only as information that the little mind of man has arrived at by making shrewd guesses of what the senses have perceived and the mind has tabulated. To a knower of the self only the realization of the Self is acceptable truth.

Verse 29

manamalar koytu mahēśa pūja, ceyyum
manujanu maṟṟoru vēla ceytiṭēṇṭā;
vanamalar koytumatallayāykil māyā-
manuvuruviṭṭumirikkil māyamāṟum.

For the man who offers his mind-flowers to worship God
there is no other work to do;
pick flowers of the forest; or, if not that,
by ever repeating the *māyā*-formula *māyā* will disappear.

To most people the world is bifurcated into the external and the internal. The internal ground is the breeding ground of imagination. Imagination can come in the form of worries, regret and remorse, revivals of memory, anxiety for the future and the creation of fantasies of future possibilities. The mind that enters the external through the organs of perception, stimulates the urge to act. Like the waves of the ocean, mind is always restless. The subject and the object stand apart as two different fields. In the wakeful state and in the dream state different kinds of interests engage the mind; it is as if mind has an obsession to be confronted with problems. Like green grass sprouting the day after a summer's rain, new thoughts, desires and worries pop up in the mind after every interlude of peace. Hardly anyone remembers that his true being is the pure existence of an ever-substantiating value that is perennially dear to him.

As the flowering phenomenality again and again offers distraction to the mind, one forgets the goal of one's life. Although the consciousness of the self is a pure effulgence of the Absolute, it shimmers like a dying spark in the darkness of nescience, and even that little spark is clothed in one's own ego and is mistaken for a personal self. The imperishable cannot be held for long in a perishable receptacle. When the vessel breaks, the wine flows out. The modalities of nature, *sattva, rajas* and *tamas,* come again and again to cause different states of consciousness.

Some people are fortunate to know that life has a meaning and that it can be lived by readjusting one's thoughts and by walking in a disciplined way. Even though these people commit themselves to such a life, the beauty or grandeur of it gives them a sense of self-righteousness which tempts them to show off their virtues. In their enthusiasm, they become salesmen of a new creed and are no longer in touch with the spirit that initially moved them. To most other people life is like a bleak desert; it has no goal, no path and no assurance of protection. Occasionally they see a mirage and become fascinated by it, but after having been disillusioned a couple of times they resort to fate. Some people think that society is at fault and all ills of the mind can be rectified by reorganizing the society. In the name of this, many utopian ideas are put forward and people get into squabbles, street fights or even wholesale war. What is the way of getting out of these anomalies of *māyā?*

Life snould be considered a sacred gift to be consecrated for the good of all. The symbolic ritual of consecration implies a supreme principle, to which its own counterpart makes a wholesale surrender, so as to gain reunion with the whole. One way of offering is to think of one's own inner moods of mind as the fresh flowers of the garden of consciousness, which can be offered to the Absolute. This is what a seer does when composing hymns of praise such as the psalms of the Bible, the hymns of the Upaniṣads and epics like the *Rāmāyana* or the *Māhābharata,* or when recording the highest allegiance that man can give to the Absolute as presented in the Holy Quran and the Talmud. A person of such dedication knows no greater value than that of the Absolute.

If such an all out dedication does not come as a spontaneous and natural expression, one should cultivate reverence for the Divine by gathering actual flowers from a garden and performing ritualistic worship. If this is done with sincerity, it might catch on and change one's life radically. It is like setting into motion a seemingly immobile flywheel. After some laborious initial rotations, when the wheel gains momentum it goes so fast that the physical weight of the wheel becomes negligible. This is the example set before others by Sri Ramakrishna.

The minds of certain people can find meaning only by gaining certitude at every step. They employ their minds diligently so as to penetrate deeper and deeper into the secrets of the phenomenal world of appearance to unravel the deep significance of life. Their aim is the visualization of ultimate truth. When they attain this goal they attain immortality.

Verse 30

jaḍamaṟivilaṟivinnu cintayillō-
tiṭukayumillaṟivennaṟiññu sarvam
viṭukil avan viśadāntaranganāy mē-
lutalil amarnnuẓalunnatilla nūnam.

Inert matter does not know; knowledge has no thought
and does not articulate; knowing knowledge to be all,
letting go, one's inner state becomes boundless;
indeed, thereafter he never suffers confined within a body.

A pin prick is enough to give intense pain. How many kinds of pain are there? Headache, earache, pains in the eye, the throat, the chest, the back and many more such items can be included in this catalogue. Certain pains are incessant and will not leave thc body once they become chronic. If a patient takes a pain-killing tablet or is given anesthesia before undergoing an operation he does not feel any pain for some time. From this, it is evident that the pain is not in the tooth or the back, but in the consciousness of sensitivity. This consciousness is neither of the body nor of the self. It is an experience that occurs where the psyche articulates in the *somos.*

Our experiences of reasoning, recalling memory, loving and hating, gratifying desire and feeling frustrated are also happening in this inner junction. These experiences are to be understood as different from the pure consciousness of the self, which is alluded to in verse 27 as the knowledge that knows itself in the dark. In the wakeful and dream experiences many coloured and preconditioned items of consciousness pass through the mind These are absent in the state of deep sleep and in the state of transcendental absorption. The absence of awareness in deep sleep is caused by a total veiling of the light of the self by *tamas,* the inertial opacity of nature. In the state of transcendental absorption, any specific forms of consciousness are absent because the activity of all three modulations of nature has ceased. This fourth state is referred to in this verse as "the boundless."

The idea of I-consciousness comes with the recognition of the individual's personal identity with the physical body and its many sensations. To move away from that identity to a pure state of absolute consciousness one has to go a long way. Various disciplines, such as study, ritualistic worship and meditation, are all employed to achieve that final goal of attaining the transcendental.

Although it is possible to go into the pure state of spiritual absorption, some vestiges of the impressions connected with the body and its needs will continue to exercise their influence as long as the body is alive. A wise man will look upon all such conditions as the inevitable appendages of physical life and will not relate such things to his pure self. Nature is phenomenal and what belongs to nature will continue to function in the body/mind complex. A wise man does not worry about it.

Verse 31

anubhavamādıyil onnirikkil allā-
tanumitiyillitu munnamakṣiyālē
anubhaviyātatukoṇṭu dharmmiyuṇṭe-
nnanumitiyāl arivīlariññiṭēṇam.

Without prior experience there is no inference;
this is not previously perceived with the eye;
therefore, know that the existence of that in which all qualities inhere
is not known by inference.

In the process of learning, the most important factor is the capacity to compare a given situation to a previous experience and to deduce from it its possible consequences. Even lower animals like cows and dogs are capable of recalling the kind disposition of a person with whom they had previously been associated, and of showing him affection. On the other hand, if pain and threat are associated with their previous encounter with that person, the animals will hastily bolt away from him, sensing a potential threat. Man has not only efficiently employed his power of recall and deductive logic, but he has also greatly enlarged their uses to his advantage. He uses several extrapolated devices; so much so, that his associations with the laws of nature and memories of. the world of calculables have become extensions of his arms and eyes for probing and experimenting beyond the outer fringes of the farthest horizons of the known universe.

The accumulation of perceptual and conceptual data has now increased so much that it cannot be all stored in the "black box" of an individual's memory. To facilitate the use of this ever-increasing data, mammoth computers are plugged into the performance desks of present day scientists and businessmen for ready reconnaissance and instantaneous inference. Even with all this, man is at present at a great disadvantage to decipher what eludes the scope of his perceptions and his calculations. What escapes attention is not a far-off nebula, hidden away in an undiscovered universe, but the very self of man that gives him his sight to see, his ear to hear, his intellect to reason, his emotions to love and a creative ego to structure a world all for himself.

Even concrete things are not the things they seem to be, they are functions and processes. We can absorb all the functions around us and statistically arrive at an approximation of the predictability of the pattern of recurring functions and processes. These functional dynamics behind all cognizable experiences are called *dharma*-s. What is it in which all these characteristics inhere? Who is it that functions? These questions cannot be easily answered. Take an orange for example, something in it is retaining its spherical shape, something is radiating its orange colour, something is shooting air capsules of its aroma into the surrounding air, a mysterious formula in it continues the alchemy of maintaining its acidic sweetness. All these are *dharma*-s and we know them. Where is the orange, the *dharmi* that is coordinating all these properties? The Buddhists found a way to solve this problem by summarily dismissing the need for a universal ground.

For the Vedantins, *dharma*, the flux of the phenomenal transformation is not the last word. They look upon *Brahman*, the Absolute Being, as the ground of all. We cannot recall this ground as a memory of the past, because it is not directly known to us through any of our previous experiences, nor can it be deduced from any of our relativistic notions. Hence, the methods of perception and inference are given up as of no use in knowing the self. The instruction given by the knowers of the Absolute is to listen to their word testimony and reflect on it.

The most important word in this verse is the "this" found at the beginning of the second line, which says "this is not previously perceived with the eye." In several verses "this" is equated with the universal ground of all knowledge. Just as the term "that" in the Upanisadic dictum "That you are," *tat tvam asi,* "this" also stands for the all-embracing universal, the *dharmī,* of which everything else is a *dharma.*

Verse 32

ar̲ivatu dharmmiyeyalla, dharmmamāmī-
yaruḷiya dharmmiyadṛśyamākayālē
dhara mutalāyavayonnumilla tānnu-
nnoru vaṭivāmar̲ivuḷḷatōrttiṭēnam.

What is known is not that in which all qualities inhere, only the qualities;
as this, in which all qualities are said to inhere, is not visible
earth and all else do not exist;
remember that there is only a form in knowledge which supports.

This body gives rise to the experience of many fictitious entities that have a transactional validity, such as names, forms, time and space. Like self-generated automatons, we breathe, think, speak and engage in many activities. There is a faculty in us called consciousness which questions, remembers, makes decisions and assumes roles. Actually, these are only properties of the living organism, they come into being with the body and with the body they perish.

Let us suppose that we dismiss from our mind all names and forms, also give up the orientation of belonging to a place at a certain time, give up the agency of action, give up identifications such as "I," "my" and "another" and don't bother to find out which is cause and what is effect. All these are functions of the mind, which is nothing but a phenomenon. Knowing this, give up the mind also. Even if one should succeed in doing all this, a persisting awareness will always remain.

This unconditional light has an existence of its own. There are no divisions in it like "before," "now" and "hereafter," it does not give rise to any kind of inductive or deductive inferences, also there is no distinction of self and non-self. One does not arrive at this knowledge by meditating upon it. It is all by itself and for itself. The true nature of that is called dhyāna.

Keeping the body still, controlling the breath, concentrating on synergic centres, observing various kinds of dietetics, fasting and praying may all help one's mind to be disciplined, but none of this will guarantee the emergence of pure consciousness in its most unconditional and pure state. All that we can say about it is that it is. It is not an act of knowing, not an object of knowledge, not even knowledge of knowledge. Any attempt to describe it will only falsify it. All that one can do about it is not do anything. It is and that is all.

Verse 33

aṟivu nijasthitiyiṅnariññiṭānāy
dhara mutalāya vibhūtiyāyi tānē
maṟiyumavasthayil ēṟi māṟi vaṭṭam–
tiriyumalātasamam tiriññitunnu.

Knowledge, to know its own nature here,
has become earth and the other elements;
spiralling up, back and turning round,
like a glowing twig it is ever turning.

That which shines by itself in the dark is the Self. It is pure knowledge. To the seed lying asleep in the earth it whispers, "Wake up, there is water, salt and nitrogen in the earth, enjoy them. Stretch your roots, there is a feast of abundance around you. Oh, sprout, break the shell, pierce through the earth and come out into the open sky. Feel the warmth and glory of the sun that comes day after day, he is the nourisher of all life. You can breathe in carbon dioxide and breathe out oxygen. Cook your food in your leaves in the sunlight by processing the carbon dioxide. Like magic out of nowhere, you can increase your girth. You can even open energy banks in the chlorophyll of the leaves, both for you and for other living creatures. Thus, you can green the earth and be the handmaid of Mother Nature to feed everyone."

When two members of the human species, a male and a female, bring their love to consummation and millions of sperms run helter-skelter, this knowledge stealthily opens the door of a single ovum and leads into it a chosen sperm to begin the magical growth of an organism. Even the man and the woman, blinded by their orgasmic ecstasy, have not the least idea of this grand manipulator who is causing the beginning of a new beginning in a dark cell, nurtured in a dark womb. Like a mathematical genius, the same knowledge computerizes the duplication and replication of the cell with such ingenuity and skill that out of an amorphous mucus emerges an ugly-looking fetus which will become a blue-eyed or dark-eyed child soon to be as dear to his parents as a priceless treasure.

The same knowledge causes a whirl in itself, turns with great speed and produces a vortex. Lo, it has become a galaxy of countless stars! Like restless eels, it swirls in the depth of the ocean as hot and cold currents and provides the earth with a temperate atmosphere that nurtures life.

The same knowledge causes strange irritations in the synapses of the brain so that a man picks up his pen and writes an epic like *The Iliad* and *The Odyssey* of Homer or *The Mahābhārata* of Vyasa. When it pleases it can create a Kalidasa or a Shakespeare without the "paraphernalia" of a university. It has its own time schedule to reveal scientific truths without making the error of bringing about an Einstein before a Galileo. This knowledge puts into the human brain mathematical equations which can guide the dexterity of human hands into creating devices that can go from the earth not only to the planets of the solar system, but also wander among the stars. It can take eternity to eternity and suddenly smash everything as if nothing had ever occurred.

Think of this vast universe with its starry heavens and the beautiful earth and no human eyes to see it with, no mind to appreciate its enormity and beauty; what a terrible waste it would be! A world without space and time, mass and energy, colour and sound, fragrance and taste and without the coordination which makes chaos into cosmos!

In short, there is only knowledge. That is the Self. That is the Oversoul. That is God. That is Goodness. That is Truth. I am that. I am the eye of the world. Oniy *is* is.

Verse 34

aranoṭiyādiyarāḷiyārnniṭum tē-
rurul atil ēriyuruṇṭiṭunnu lōkam;
arivil anādiyatāy naṭanniṭum tan-
tiruviḷayaṭāl itennariññiṭēṇam.

Mounted on the rotating wheels of a chariot which have half-moments and such for spokes,
the world rolls on;
know this to be the beginningless divine sport
that is ever going on in knowledge.

Once there was a scholastic theologian called St. Augustine. He was a world renowned philosopher and a Christian mystic. In his *Confessions* he meditates on time and says: "Does not my soul most truly confess unto Thee, that I do measure times? Do I then measure, O my God, and know not what I measure? I measure the motion of a body in time; and the time itself do I not measure? Or could I indeed measure the motion of a body how long it were, and in how long a space it could come from this place to that, without measuring the time in which it is moved? This same time then, how do I measure? Do we by a shorter time measure a longer, as by the space of a cubit, the space of a rood?"

In this prolonged meditation on time he became more and more confused about it and he finally came to the conclusion that there is no past or future, but only a fraction of a passing moment called the present.

The past is only a name for the recall of our memory, the future is the name for our anticipation. How do memory and anticipation become time? The Indian concept of the present is that which can be measured mentally or literally. We can measure space and objects in space, but we will be frustrated if we try to measure time; it always slips away. Even the whole of the moment does not present itself as a complete unit.

Isn't it strange that a universe with a history of countless billions of years is comprehended in all its seeming infinitude within the fraction of a vanishing moment? Guru humorously compares the world to a jolly ride of a mammoth chariot, whose motion depends entirely on the transient half moment which a spoke takes to move.

Well, the world may be a fleeting phenomenon; should that make the self also fleeting? The self is pure knowledge. However, in the experience of most people, mind becomes as restless as this rotating and revolving universe. It is hard to control the mind. There are, however, occasions when the mind is restful. Visualize such a state. When you are at peace with yourself, mind is like an expanse of consciousness. In such blessed moments one does not say it is gone or it is coming, there is no sense of time. The breadth and the depth are also not differentiated. Peace reigns supreme, there is no limit to it. In our imagination we can soar high, and with equal ease we can dive deep.

In that knowledge which is devoid of the consciousness of space and time, a little bubble of motivation comes to burst on the surface. It causes a small ripple no bigger than a ring. One ripple begets another, each bigger and wider than the other. Very soon the mind becomes a stormy sea, it becomes eventful. In this deluge one sits on the crest of a tidal wave and laments for the lost world of peaceful harmony. The anticipatory dream of the future comes as well. Things do not turn out as expected and that brings frustration. Life appears like an autumn leaf fluttering in the wind, one trembles with fear. The only knowledge in that moment is a sense of helplessness. The magnitude of the self has now shrunk into a torn bit of consciousness, it gets caught in the eddy of uncertainty. Where is the goal? What is life's achievement? Nothing is known. In frustration one gives up all hope and sits down to rest his tired limbs. Then from somewhere, like a gentle breeze, peace returns. The restless world changes once again into an infinitude of silence.

What is all this? Maybe God is playing. Life is a divine sport, and eternity rides on the wheels of fleeting moments.

Verse 35

oru patināyiramāditēyar onnāy
varuvatu pōle varum vivēkavṛtti
aṟivine mūṭumanitya māyayāmī-
yiruḷineyīrneẓumādi sūryyan atrē.

Like ten thousand suns coming all at once,
the modulation of discrimination arises;
the veil of transcience covering knowledge is *māyā;*
tearing this away, the primal sun alone shines.

We see before our eyes an enchanting world of exquisite beauty, which can also become horrid, vulgar and threatening. When our senses are possessed by the spirit of that world, mind becomes infatuated or hysterical. Similarly, there is a world within us; it is of fantasy and imagination. Sometimes it leads to the imaginary mansion of the fool's paradise and feeds our pleasure-seeking mind with a Barmecidal feast such as Alice's tea party with the Mad Hatter. Some unfortunate people wake up from such an illusion only to be caught in this never-ending nightmare; to them life is a pool of tears. With a smile of indifference the self sits unconcerned between these two worlds called the external and the internal.

The self is pure knowledge which transcends all specific notions. It is the supernal sun that shines in the firmament of consciousness. It is not the knowledge of anything, but the being of knowledge. It is the unlit lamp that shines as the soul of everything, which never becomes extinguished even if the body perishes. It knows no transformation. It is the secret of *aum.* It is the certitude which allows no riddles or doubts. It is the witnessing consciousness that is silent by nature. It is the golden link that connects everything to give unitive understanding. It is the Absolute that transcends all the three modalities of nature. Its field is not divided into any regions in space or divisions in time. It sustains the Blessed Ones with the blissful nectar of divine wisdom. It is an all-filling symphony which opens the eye of wisdom. It is the Primal Glory which knows no modulation.

Even though half-moments give birth to name and form, space and time, actor and enjoyment of action, cause and effect, the universal and the particular, the five elements, the three modalities, the triple states of consciousness, the six-fold transformations of life and the duality of pain and pleasure, it takes only one quarter of a moment for all these aggregates to be blown up into a conflagration of dazzling light, as if ten thousand suns had suddenly come into being as an all-embracing consciousness.

This is not just wishful thinking. It happened to Siddhartha Gautama when after five years of fruitless search and mortification of the body, he sat under a bo tree to give up his life in desperation. In a single flash he became the Awakened One, the blessed Buddha. It happened to the son of a Nazarene carpenter called Jesus. He stood in the Jordan to be baptized by a crazy man called John, who described himself as "the cry in the wilderness," and like lightning the heavens broke open and the spirit of God entered Jesus and made him the Christ, the Light of the world. A simple man who did not nurture his brain by going to any school, but did humble service to a pious Arabian widow, once sheltered himself in the cool shade of a cave. There he had an encounter with the one Self which is behind all selves. It commanded him to read the divine revelations. Poor Muhammad Mustafa lamented his fate and pleaded his ignorance of the written word. Once again the miracle happened, the ignorant Muhammad became the wisest of all prophets in the wink of an eye, and lo, he chanted to the world the nectar-like *suras* of the Holy Quran. An illiterate priest of West Bengal became infatuated with his love for a stone image of Kali. Sri Ramakrishna wanted the stone to become flesh. The Divine Will that once transformed the Word into flesh came to his rescue and transformed the clod of his mind into the blissful ecstasy of the highest possible realization. In a mountain cave of South India, where the three oceans meet, Narayana Guru lived, befriending a cobra and a tiger as he found human nature no better than that of brutes. After years of penance in that solitary cave he suddenly awakened to the one Reality that makes everything real and precious. No one is more chosen than any other. All these masters were human beings, just like you and I. Tomorrow it can be our turn.

Verse 36

ar̲ivinu śaktiyanantamuṇṭitellā-
mar̲utiyiṭām 'sama' 'anya' yennivaṇṇam
iru pirivāy itil anya sāmyamārnnu-
ḷḷuruvil amarnnu teḷiññuṇarnniṭēṇam.

The power of knowledge is endless;
the end of all this can be marked as "sameness" and "the other";
thus, in this way, there are two divisions; in this, merging the other with sameness,
one should remain awake to that clear state of being.

When we hear the English word "knowledge" what comes to our mind is a passive idea, such as that of a reflected image in the mirror. Guru, however, is not using the word *arivu* (knowledge) in such a passive sense, it is both passive and dynamic. Words like awareness, consciousness and knowledge refer only to partial aspects of that great dynamic whole which includes within it the conscious and the unconscious, the potential and the actual, the transcendent and the immanent, the creative and the created. In the present verse knowledge is to be understood as all this. In that sense, what is there other than knowledge? The simplest form of knowledge is the awareness of the I-consciousness. When a person says "I am," what he says is: "I know that I am." In this sentence "I" comes twice. Is the first "I" different from the second "I"? And what is the difference between "I am" and "I know"? The first "I" is a postulate to be examined. The examination is performed by knowing it. Knowing is a process. The culmination of the process is restated as a verified "I." The verification is that it exists. Its existence is emphasized here as "I am." The awareness of the I-consciousness is a very simple pulsation of an idea, there cannot be anything more simple than that, yet in that simple act of awareness, there is a presentation, a scrutiny and a judgement.

Irrespective of all these movements or modifications of consciousness, there prevails a pure knowledge which is at once transcendent and immanent. If this is recognized, then there is only knowledge. It is possible to postulate the existence of this world without our ever knowing it, but even for that negative postulation, one has to exercise knowledge. It is knowledge that reveals to us that we have no knowledge of certain things and we have knowledge of certain other things. Knowledge hides itself and experiences forgetfulness or ignorance. Like a magician, knowledge restores what is forgotten and reveals what seems not to have been known before.

Knowledge projects a whole world of name, form, and intense activity. With the same ease it pulls that world aside as a chimerical dream. From the day of our birth, knowledge has flowed in from all sides, like rivers flowing into an ocean. Just like the ocean that never overflows, knowledge remains unfilled and there is plenty of room to receive more and more knowledge. It is never satiated, nor is it ever tired of producing variegations.

When, as ignorant persons, we listen to others, we only understand if we are told words that correspond to concepts that already exist within ourselves. No new knowledge ever comes from outside, but by making permutations and combinations of our innate knowledge, we are led to believe that we know new things every day. Knowledge is a magician showing a grand magic to itself. It is both baffled and gratified.

Without knowledge we cannot desire anything. We need knowledge to know the means to fulfill our desires. The right knowledge to fulfill is experienced as the dynamics of action. This action and knowledge are not two things. The propensity of motivation, the power of comprehension, and the dynamics of action are all to be understood as a power of infinite magnitude. In its collective and universal nature it is called *sama,* the same. We live that knowledge at the transactional and empirical levels. Empirical experience comes through the senses. We see different objects with our eyes, we hear different things with our ears; in the empirical world one knowledge is differentiated from another. There the knower becomes the subject and the known becomes the object of knowledge, thus knowledge becomes compartmentalized. This aspect of knowledge is called *anya,* the other.

A contemplative should learn to transcend both the *sama* and the *anya.* When we see a garland we notice the harmonious structuring of the flowers that make it a whole. We can appreciate the colour, fragrance and the beauty of each individual flower, and we can also see the garland as a whole. It should be the same in life too; we can be in the thick of it, enjoying and experiencing every detail of it, and all the same, we can also experience the most serene unchanging inner beatitude of the supreme knowledge which is providing for all variegated experiences.

Verse 37

viṣamatayārnneẓumanya vennu koḷvān
viṣamamakhaṇḍa vivēka śaktiyennyē;
viṣamaye vennatināl vivēkamākum
viṣaya virōdhiniyōṭanaññiṭēṇam.

The other is replete with difficulty;
and it is hard to win over without the power to discriminate the unbroken;
having won over the difficult,
attain to that discrimination which is opposed to sense interests.

We cannot go to sleep by deliberation. Sleep has to come from within us as a spontaneous fading out of our consciousness. Of course, we can put our bodies into an inert state by taking sleeping pills, but that is like committing temporary suicide. We cannot force ourselves to love anyone. Love is a tender emotion that comes naturally from our innermost self. All we can do is create a situation in which love can be nurtured. We cannot make our mind concentrate by applying brute compulsion. When a deep interest is stimulated in us, concentration comes as a natural consequence. Mind becomes peaceful only when its modulations slowly cease.

It is not easy to extricate the mind from its entanglements and free it so it can feel its oneness with the universal ground of consciousness. Each stimulus brings with it a specific form of pain and pleasure. It is not natural for the mind to transcend its affectivity so as to always remain established in the blissful state of the universal self. Worries come with restrospective remorse or prospective anxiety. Discursive ratiocination drags the mind along idle forms of reasoning. Imagination haunts the mind and creates fantasies of all sorts. Actions sow their seeds and create chain reactions, many other diseases can bring physical and mental ailments. Even a pinprick can upset the mind. To reclaim the serenity of the soul from all these disturbances is a very difficult feat. No man is left alone by the society of which he is an integral part. In fact, society may drive a person mad, or compel him to commit suicide.

There is no end to it, we can go on and on cataloguing the potentials of *anya.*

The antidote for all the above-mentioned evils is our power of discrimination. In our meditation on verse 35, we have seen how the grace of wisdom and discrimination came to the Buddha, Jesus Christ, the prophet Muhammad, Sri Ramakrishna, and Narayana Guru like ten thousand suns rising all at once in the sky of their consciousness.

We experience this world as several unrelated fragmentary bits of effects even though they have all emanated from one single cause. At the very beginning of these hundred verses of self-instruction we are advised to withhold our senses and prostrate before the supreme cause of both the inner and the outer world. In verse 13, we are advised to turn to the God who has transcended the three modalities of nature and to worship him by offering the blossoms of our mind. Only by cultivating an all-absorbing love for the Absolute will we be able to work out our final release from the compulsive obsession of *anya.*

Verse 38

palavidhamāy aṟiyunnatanyayonnāy
vilasuvatām samayennu mēlilōtum
nilayeyaṟiññu nivarnnu sāmyamēlum
kalayil aliññu kalarnnirunniṭēṇam.

What is known as many is the other,
and that which shines forth as one is sameness;
having known the state, which is going to be spoken of, and attained release,
remain dissolved and blended in the state of sameness.

People have different tastes and temperaments. Even in one family people like to dress differently, eat differently and amuse themselves differently. Lack of agreement in opinions and personal values causes constant friction. When husband and wife adopt different life styles and begin to fight, they make their home a hell for themselves as well as their children.

In the Gospel according to Luke, Jesus says: "Suppose ye that I am come to give peace on earth? I tell you Nay; but rather division; For from henceforth there shall be five in one house divided, three against two, and two against three. The father shall be divided against the son, and the son against the father; the mother against the daughter and the daughter against the mother..." To verify the truth of this we can find any number of examples.

There is however a way to overcome this anomaly, and that is by cultivating unitive understanding. The *Bhagavad Gita* gives the following instructions:

> Such a yogi, verily, of calmed mind, of pacified passion, who has become the Absolute, and free from all dross, comes to supreme happiness.
> Ever uniting thus the Self, that yogi, rid of dross, having contact with the Absolute, enjoys easily happiness that is ultimate.
> One whose Self is united by yoga sees the Self as abiding in all beings

> and all beings as abiding in the Self, everywhere seeing the same.
> He who sees Me everywhere, and sees everything in Me, to him I am not lost and he is not lost to Me. That yogi who honours Me as abiding in all beings, established in unity, remaining as he may, in every (possible) way, he abides in Me.
> By establishing an analogy with the Self, he who sees equality everywhere, O Arjuna, whether (in) pleasant or painful (situations), he is considered a perfect yogi.

Mind does not allow itself to be controlled so easily. It can become weird and cause tempests, but there are moments when the mind is calm. These occasions should be used to direct it to the universal oneness of the self which animates everything. When the mind is calm it should be taught to become compassionate and get into fraternal commitments. If we do so repeatedly, the mind can be absolved from its hysteria and ultimately one can find one's full relief.

Verse 39

aruḷiya śaktikaḷettuṭarnnu ranṭām
pirivivayil samatan viśēṣamēkam;
virati varā viṣamā viśēṣamonni-
ttaramiva ranṭu tarattil āyiṭunnu.

To continue, of these forces just mentioned,
the second division, sameness, is of one quality,
while for the first, the difficult, there is no end to its qualities;
thus, these are of two kinds.

All experiences of the wakeful state are knowledge of one form or another. The dream state is also knowledge. The recalling of the deep sleep experience indicates the latent aspect of knowledge in deep sleep. When a yogi sits in a state of absorption, transcending time and the knowledge of all names and forms, he still has knowledge of a certain kind. Sometimes knowledge is indescribable, and there is no need to communicate it to anyone. In that state also, it is knowledge. The knowledge in all these cases has only one quality, it is its self-luminosity. It shines by itself and it illuminates all objects of knowledge.

When light illuminates something, it does not change into anything other than light. Similarly, when knowledge becomes an experience, it does not become anything other than knowledge; even in that process it looks as if the one is becoming many. No one can say how many objects light can illuminate. In the same manner, there is no end to the capacity of knowledge for making things known. We only have one mind with which to know everything. It goes on arguing with endless reasons on countless issues. Its observations are infinite. The data it gathers and installs as memory is fabulous. It is capable of sharpening its wits to mathematical precision, and it can also accumulate clouds of confusion that can make its owner go crazy. Thus, its indiscernible nature qualifies itself in infinite forms.

If we turn away from objects of knowledge to the knower, we see a shimmering consciousness there which, as it goes on, alternates between its two modes. It continuously says, "This is me," "This is what I know." When it says, "This is me," what is the "this"? That is knowledge. When it says, "This is what I know," what is that "this"? That is also knowledge.

From childhood's first articulations to the very end of life, one will go on saying, "This is me." Will there ever be any difference in that subjective recognition of me? No, it will always be the same. Is it the same that is known on different occasions? No, it is always different. Is it not strange that one's knowledge remains changeless throughout one's life, and yet it is changing all through?

Verse 40

samayilumanyayilum sadāpi vanni-
nnamaruvatuṇṭatatin viśēṣa śakti
amitayarākilumāke raṇṭivaṟṟin-
bhramakalayāl akhilam pramēyamākum.

In sameness and in the other each one's
qualifying force always comes and becomes established;
by the fluctuating function of these two,
which comprises all, everything becomes the object of awareness.

"I shall give the meaning of this verse." "Let us learn the all-embracing wisdom of the great seers." In these two sentences there are two different kinds of emphasis. In the first instance, the subject "I" makes a specific reference to the person concerned, and thus differentiates him from all others. The object of that sentence refers to a particular verse, also differentiating it from other items of knowledge. Thus the main note of this sentence is *anya.* In the second statement "I" changes into the all-inclusive "us." The object matter is also an inclusive one. Thus, the dominant note in this sentence is *sama.* In our daily transactions we adopt both these stands. *Anya* is personal, specific and ego-centred. *Sama* is impersonal, general and altruistic. If *anya* is analytic, *sama* is synthetic. When we understand a person with reference to his physical body, he is different from others in form, colour, the tenor of his voice, his individual taste and temperament, his moods and behavioural patterns. These are only a few distinctive marks, but we can go on enumerating many more distinctions. When a thing is analyzed into its simpler elements, the thing changes and begins to vanish. When an atom is finally blasted, it becomes a destructive force. Thus, the power of specificity is unaccountably large and varied.

When all the limbs are put together we have a body. When all the structural and functional aspects of the body become pronounced as a personality we have an individual. When individuals associate themselves as a corporate whole we have a society. When all societies are brought under one universal group we have a species, and when all species are brought into the homogenous whole we have a genus. Absolute knowledge includes everything. Our personal knowledge is always moving between the most specific and the most generic. If a person is absorbed in his non-differentiated knowledge of the Absolute, there is no known or knower to know anything. There the operational aspect of knowledge has no significance. When an individual becomes obsessed with one single item of knowledge that stupefies him to the point of madness and thus brings about a malfunction of the agency of the knower in him.

Fortunately knowledge does not remain static either in its specific modes or in its universal mode. It is natural for man to shrink into himself and act as a psychological entity. With the same ease, he can also expand his consciousness and become an integral part of the cosmos. Thus, life is a pulsation of consciousness with the alternating emphases of *anya* and *sama.* Guru describes these two functions as the operational instrumentality of the specific and the universal. A contemplative can detach his witnessing awareness and transcend both these aspects.

Verse 41

> *"itu kuṭam" ennatil ādyamām "ite" nnu-*
> *ḷḷatu viṣamā; kuṭamō viśēṣamākum;*
> *mati mutalāya mahēndra jālamuṇṭā-*
> *vatinitutān karuvennu kaṇṭiṭēṇam.*

> **"This is a pot"; in** that, what comes first, "this,"
> is the difficult to discern; pot is its qualifying predicate;
> for intellect and such *mahēndra* magic to manifest,
> this itself becomes the *karu*; thus one should see.

Mind always begins to function with questions such as "What is this?" "How is this?" etcetera. These questions open the door to the world of the unknown and the unconscious. We have already pointed out that this questioning aspect of consciousness is called *manas.* These questions are followed by the emergence of several associated memories. Memories are basically of a conceptual order. Every form that we see and every word we hear becomes related to a concept. We do not notice any lapse between the occurrence of a perception and its corresponding conception. The emergence of a concept that relates to a name or form is instantaneous and spontaneous. Concepts remain hidden in the unconscious even before they illuminate a percept. The question that arises in the mind is an occasion to relate a concept or a percept, or to interrelate two concepts so as to make a complete inferential judgement. When a person says, "This is a pot," it already implies a question such as "What is this?" When it is instantaneously answered as, "This is a pot," it is automatically accompanied by an evaluation of that pot from a pragmatic point of view.

When it occurs to the mind, "This is a pot" is no longer a thing outside or inside. Mind locates a thing by psychologically conceiving time and space. The idea of the concrete has its corresponding concepts in the mind. As an alchemy, the sensory stimulus undergoes a transformation by which the physical reality of the pot and the psychological awareness of it are fused into a transactional verity. It is impossible to say how much of it is physical or non-physical.

"This," which is found both in the question, "What is this?" and in the answer, "This is a pot," does not give any idea until it is qualified, and hence it is called indiscernible. It is the common source of all variants. In the present verse it is called *karu,* which can be translated as "substance," "yolk," or "mould." This occurs in the very first verse of this book. Then we were instructed to turn to this primordial substance with an attitude of adoration and know it to be the divine source of everything. In the present verse we come into a greater intimacy with "this" as both the revealing and the illuminating exponent of all knowledge. When we do not have the consistent recognition of its divine nature the translucency of our ego comes between the illuminating source and the illuminated knowledge. As a result of this veiling principle of the ego's ignorance every item of knowledge becomes a magical transfiguration.

Verse 42

"idamarive" nnatil ādyamām "ite" nnu-
ḷḷatu sama; tante viśēṣamānu bōdham;
mati mutalāyavayokke māri mēl sad-
gati varuvān itinebbhajicciṭēṇam.

"This is knowledge"; in that, what comes first, "this,"
is sameness; its qualifying predicate is awareness;
for intellect and all such to vanish, and for the true path to come,
this should be meditated on.

This self is the Absolute. This body is perishable. This is truth. This is untruth. In all this, "this" indicates that there is something to be considered. IN all these atomic sentences the word "this" is the nucleus. When "this" is presented by itself it makes no definite sense. In the sentence, "This is a pot," "pot" qualifies "this." The predicative aspect is therefore called *viśeṣa.* "What is this?" is the problem-raising element of mind; its complementarity comes from the predicating judgement, "This is a pot." The faculty that complements the mind is the intellect. Mind goes on asking questions, and the intellect goes on answering them.

As "this" is a common term used to indicate or suggest the presence of everything to be known, it has an inner homogeneity. For this reason it is called *sama,* or sameness. In the sentence "This is knowledge," "this" is *sama* and "knowledge" is its qualifying predicate. Before predication the specific properties of things and ideas remain hidden in the unknown or the unconscious respectively. Knowledge has three functions: it invites attention, it relates the subject to the predicate, it grasps and retains the meaning.

It is the intellect which reveals to the ego the emotional value potency of the predicated specific property of whatever is presented to consciousness. The revelation of values causes intrigue in the total personality. The individual is most likely impelled to react to an actual situation or a potential situation indicated by the value significance of the experience in question. We have two options in such situations. One is to approach the subject from an ego-centred angle and initiate a chain of action/reaction complex. By assuming that posture the knower becomes both an enjoyer and an actor. The othei possibility is to look at the issue unitively from the passive standpoint of a universal spectator. Although being a spectator of the passing show of life may bring a general sense of appreciation, it does not produce any compulsions to take upon oneself the role of an actor. Consequently, such an attitude promotes release from role playing situations. A contemplative who aspires to peace and harmony is recommended here to cultivate a unitive understanding of the purport of "this," which comes to the surface of the mind like never-ending ripples of curiosity.

Verse 43

prakṛti piṭiccu cuẓaṟṟiṭum prakāram
sukṛtikaḷ pōlumahō cuẓanniṭunnu!
vikṛti viṭunnatināyi vēlaceyvī-
lakṛti phalāgrahamaṟṟaṟiññiṭēṇam.

Even those of good action are caught by nature
and whirled round in vicious circles;
one should know that non-action does not bring release from perverted action,
only the non-desire for the fruit of action.

When an ego-centred man sees an object of pleasure, an interest to gratify some desire connected with that object is triggered in him. Even when he is not confronted with such a possibility he will hatch out plans to find means and ends that will take him from one pleasure pursuit to another. Occasionally he is cornered by mishaps that makes him scared. Even when he is on secure grounds, the paranoia of some unknown danger lying in ambush in the near future will haunt his imagination. It is easy to see how such a person becomes a victim of the enigmatic uncertainties of nature. When we say "nature" what we mean is not the hills and dales, or the sky and ocean, but the nature of our own personality structure. Each individual is like a lump of inertial darkness concealing within himself various charges of dynamite of varying strength, all geared to blast off at different times. To make this picture complete we should imagine an imprisoned splendour in the dark mass which is in resonance with the divine source of all manifestations. By putting together the bright, the dark and the kinetic we get a rough picture of our nature.

Those people who are liberal-minded and have altruistic ideals see the sameness of all and are moved with compassion to do good for others. They are certainly different from a self-centred hedonist, but, in spite of their good intentions, they too get trapped in the snares of the collective function of the triple modalities of the society to which they belong. They cultivate love, compassion and fellowship, and they initiate actions for the actualization of these ideas. Their watchword is "do good." It is with great sincerity that they commit themselves to carry out enormous duties so as to bring welfare to mankind.

Every good work is foreshadowed by a resistance. Like light casts a shadow, so the good intentions of an altruistic person rouse suspicion and fear in the mind of people who are either engaged in some act of exploitation or are afraid of losing their vested interest. To much the same proportion, the good man's intention inspires hope and good will in people of like nature. Thus, what one individual initiates develops into a teamwork opposed by reactionary forces. If the good man is only an idealist who is simply motivated by the desire to do good and who has no insight with which to discern the phenomenal world as a superimposition of the collective will on an unchanging transcendent being, he will take all the rebuffs and backfire as personal attacks hurled at him by a section of the ungrateful society for which he has made his best sacrifices. This will bring despair and frustration. It is sad to see so many patriots, politicians and welfare workers live their old age in loneliness, cursing their fate after wasting their precious lives in the pursuit of empty ideals and fruitless dreams. Thus, a man of good work finally becomes cynical of action.

We have, however, examples of another model, the ones who bring substantial good to the world without ever losing their cheer, courage or hope. They are dedicated people with consecrated souls who do not look for the fruition of any benefits in a kingdom of God that is yet to come. They transcend time and live in the eternal present. If they do good actions it is not because they want to be good, but because they have so transformed into goodness that only goodness can come from them.

Nature and spirit are not two things. A properly harmonized nature is the best expression of the spirit. The Buddha, who lived 2500 years ago, is just as vital, moving and forceful today in the minds of millions of people. The good work started in the Deer Park at Varanasi twenty-six centuries ago is still going on, transforming the lives of people.

Realizing truth is becoming beautiful. Beauty is another word for goodness, and goodness prevails where relativistic disparity and exclusion become nullified. It is for this reason that the Absolute is praised in the Quran as Allah, the beneficent and the merciful.

Verse 44

pala mata sāravumēkamennu pārā-
tulakil orānayil andhar ennapōle
pala vidha yukti paraññu pāmaranmā-
ralavatu kaṇṭalayātamarnnitēnam.

The many faiths have but one essence;
not seeing this, in this world, like the blind men and the elephant,
many kinds of reasoning are used by the unenlightened who become distressed;
having seen this, without being disturbed, remain steadfast.

If we hide a pot behind a screen and ask someone to identify it, that person, unaware of the hidden object, might make a number of conjectures. To qualify "this" in the question "What is this?" Guru tells us in verse 41 that "this" is the primal cause for fabricating the ideational world of the intellect. The consciousness implied can, however, also function unitively and can easily comprehend how a universal beingness always remains as the transcendent essence of everything. To such a consciousness "this" is the unifying element of all.

The original vision and inspiration associated with the founders of all great religions can be traced to people who are fully realized masters, such as Janaka and Yajnavalkya of the Upaniṣads, the Buddha, Mahavira of the Jains, the Christ, Lao Tzu and the Prophet. What they have seen and experienced is beyond words and certainly beyond the comprehension of a relativistically oriented mind. When these great masters disseminated their wisdom, whatever trickle came in the form of articulated words was half lost because of the poverty of language and misunderstood because the recipients' minds were not as enlightened as those of their masters.

As a result of this, feuds and conflicts arose among the congregates of all masters. For the purposes of social security and political advantage the followers of all major religions got themselves organized. Several times the world has been bathed in the blood of religious dissidents, and even the word religion is now looked upon with horror and suspicion by the people who care for the brotherhood of mankind.

Spiritual experience is not arrived at as a logical conclusion of inductive or deductive reasoning. It is a wholesome transformation of all the dissonance of nature in one's personality into a harmonious resonance to the truth, beauty and goodness in all. Although reason is an excellent tool for making a unitive understanding beneficial to all concerned, it has no potential of its own to make a person enlightened.

When we are confronted by a raving fanatic, it causes disquiet in our minds and, as if in a state of hypnosis, even the most liberally minded man is tempted to take up a cudgel to defend himself. Only those who are well established in the universality of the all-embracing sameness can hold their peace and remain unruffled on such provocative occasions. When the world around us goes mad with religious factions and separatism unitive wisdom is a panacea.

Verse 45

oru matamanyanu nindyamonnil ōtum-
karuvaparante kaṇakki nūnamākum;
dharayil itinte rahasyamonnutān e-
nnar̲ivaḷavum bhramamennar̲iññiṭēṇam.

One faith is despicable to another;
the *karu* described in one is defective in another's estimation;
in the world the secret of this is one alone;
know that confusion prevails until it is known to be thus.

It is not compulsory that everyone should have a religion. Many people think they have no religious convictions or are indifferent to religion, but on closer scrutiny it can be seen that each person has his own personal convictions, preferences and habitual choices. Although these are not necessarily religious, the essence of all this implies one's way of seeking and finding his or her personal notion of happiness. Only part of this personal style is regulated by any rational thinking. Prejudices, instinctive urges, unconscious defence mechanisms and even pathological traits can be part of one's built-in personal attitude. However structured or haphazard this personal life style might be, it affects one's mode of dressing, food habits, behavioural patterns, social affiliations, conformity to customs, goal motivations and mode of thinking.

Among the conformists we see organized groups like Buddhists, Christians, Muslims, Vaishnavites, Saivites, Sikhs, freethinkers and communists. They indoctrinate their children at an early age. It is almost impossible for a child to grow up in the human society without being adversely or favourably affected by both the vertical and the horizontal pressures of a continuing society. As Henri Bergson puts it, the parent is an office which has the authority to regulate the child. Most children prefer to take the path of least resistance and thus they easily succumb to traditional prejudices. In all fairness, one should admit, however, that it is also possible for a child to learn from his or her parents the traditional wisdom of his forefathers. Whichever way the mind is fashioned and bent, it becomes mature and somewhat consolidated for all times well before they come to adulthood. The individual upbringing gives to everyone a yardstick which is practically of no use when it is to be applied to a life situation not familiar to one's own accepted pattern. In the mind of most people this creates an attitude of, "I am OK and you are not OK."

If a turtle goes for a walk on dry land, when he returns to his pool to share his experience with the friendly fish of the pond they will laugh at his stupidity for saying he was walking on land instead of swimming. The greatest curse of mankind is its confusion of terms. Even people speaking the same language have difficulties in understanding each other because each person uses the private metaphors of his own religious convictions.

Controversy arises between doctrinists of religion in defining the highest truth each wants to uphold. The Guru uses the term *karu* in a most comprehensive sense, which can cover several aspects of the Absolute such as the all transcendent, the primeval cause, the substance that evolves into all moulds, the archetypes and the overall norm of all evaluations.

Only a wise man sees that the essence of all search is the love for happiness. Those who know this transcendental essence remain calm and smile with compassion when their fellow men brandish weapons of threat in the confused clang of endless rivalry and competition.

Wherever the word "this" *(itu)* comes it should be specially looked into to see if it is used in the sense of "the difficult." The *karu* spoken of above is the Absolute, which at no time is fully discernible. "This," which refers directly to the *karu,* offers the greater challenge to any seeker to comprehend its meaning clearly. The term *dhara* used in this verse stands in marked contrast with *ulaku* in the previous verse. The roots of *dhara* and *dharma* are the same. Discerning meaning correctly is a must in a world of consistent meaning (*dhara*) and it is only optional in a world of opinions (*ulaku*).

Verse 46

porutu jayippatasāddhyamonninōṭo-
nnoru matavum porutāl otuṅṅuvīla;
para matavādiyitōrttiṭāte pāẓē
porutu poliññiṭumenna buddhi vēṇam.

By fighting it is impossible to win;
by fighting one another no faith is destroyed;
one who argues against another's faith, not recognizing this,
fights in vain and perishes; this should be understood.

A religion cannot be brushed away as just somebody's mere opinion. When we look at the followers, we see that major religions are giving them the inspiration to live meaningful lives. Religion consoles many aching hearts. It encourages people to organize themselves into becoming productive corporations. It promotes art and culture. Over centuries it grows into a tradition that shapes the destiny of millions of people. All this is possible only because religion has within it the fountain source of perennial values. We do not know how deep the roots of our personal beliefs are. We are only vaguely aware of the goal to which we are moving and our potentials are not fully assessed or estimated. In short, what we know about ourselves is only very little.

The religion of a people is certainly greater than the wishes, convictions and dreams of a single individual. To estimate the magnitude of religion in general, let us turn our attention to two major religions which have been going strongly through millennia in spite of many adverse forces that tried to crush them; these are Judaism and Vedic Hinduism. The inner structure of the Kabbalah, which contains the mystical essence of Judaism, is represented by the sacred tree of *sephiroth.*

Judaism rests on the ever adorable values of wisdom, reason, knowledge, greatness, strength, beauty, eternity, majesty, principle and sovreignty (*Chokmah, Binah, Daath, Gedulah, Geburah, Tiphereth, Netzach, Hod, Yesod, Malkuth*).

This can be compared to the Vedic tree described in chapter 15 of the *Bhagavad Gita.* Its roots are above and the branches grow downward and sideways. The leaves sprouting on these branches are the meters of the Vedic chants. Its branches are the proliferations of the three modalities of nature. The lower branches produce roots which go down into the ground and keep the tree steadfast. The intertwining of these roots is the *karma* of the collective masses which makes mankind an interrelated matrix. This tree has no form, no beginning or end, and no one knows its real formations. This tree can be transcended only with detachment.

The values glorified in Judaism and the symbolic picture presented of Hinduism appear in every major religion in one form or other. If someone fancies that these religions could be blotched away by sheer force, he would be attempting the impossible. Marx, Freud and Nietzsche dreamt of the possibility of the withering away of religion, but instead of bringing about the death of the present religions, they only added three new offshoots. The more you fight religion, the more virile and invigorated it becomes.

In India religion is called *dharma* because it sustains all the traditionally preserved essential values of life. Motivation to act comes from the embedded seeds of value aspirations. An individual, who is on his march from his cradle to his grave, has within his biologic, psychologic and moral ingenuity several long-tried devices implanted by Mother Nature to protect him from all possible dangers through which he has to wend his way. When several such individuals become a closely knit social organism they develop a culture and tradition that becomes unassailable. For this reason religion can never be annihilated, though it has been overpowered for short periods in history.

The way of the Absolute is all-encompassing. By accepting the validity of another person's faith, we can avoid the exaggeration of its emotional impact and defensive reactions. By appreciating and imbibing the essentials of another religion we will only discover the greater and hidden truth of our own religion, hence it is foolish to promote exclusiveness in religious attitudes. Unitive understanding enables one to appreciate that the essence of all religions is the same.

Verse 47

oru matamākuvatinnurappatellā-
varumitu vādikaḷ ārumōrkkuvīla;
paramatavādamoẓiññа paṇḍitanmā-
raṟiyumitinte rahasyaminnaśeṣam.

To become of one faith is what everyone speaks of;
this the proselytizers do not recognize;
wise men, freed of objections to another's faith,
know this secret in full.

"Hear what I say." "This is the whole truth." "What is your opinion?" We often hear such remarks in the course of conversations. Conversations, letters, books, magazine articles and public speeches are all intended to bring about unity of ideas.

During the Conference of World Religions convened by Narayana Guru, he gave the delegates the following watchword: "We are here to know and to let know, not to argue and win." A person wanting to know envisages the value of another man's vision. His preparedness to listen paves the way for acceptance and consequently unity arises. When a person wants to share his knowledge or spiritual experience he already desires the well-being of another. The essence of all religions is equally precious to those who have no hang-ups such as "my religion" and "your religion."

Until recently, if a Hindu went to a restaurant in North India the waiter would ask the cook to supply a "beautiful tea," but if a Muslim should go to the same restaurant, the same waiter would ask the same cook to supply a "plain tea." In both instances the cook would produce the same tea, but in a cup and saucer of floral design for the Hindu and in a plain cup and saucer for the Muslim. This was to assure the Hindu that he was not using the same utensils as the Muslim and vice versa. This is only one of the mildest idiosyncrasies born of separatism. The most grotesque and catastrophic versions are the eruptions of war between India and Pakistan, Israel and Arab countries, and the constant clash between the Catholics and the Protestants in Northern Ireland, to mention only a few well-known examples.

Bertrand Russell puts his finger right on the crux of the whole issue when he says that all differences are born of the semantic ambiguity which does not make clear a word meaning. A recent catastrophe, erupted from such a semantic issue, happened because of the lack of clarity in defining democracy and communism. The Marxists called themselves social democrats until Lenin decided to call his creed communism. To decide the operational meaning of these two words, the United States of America sent at least half-a-million young men to the marshy fields of Vietnam to kill or get killed. Ultimately the whole of Vietnam came under the label of communism and the semantic issue continues unresolved.

Religion or ideology becomes more than a curse to people when politicians offer themselves to be the efficient interpreters of high ideals.

The Christian proselytizer thinks that if all people are brought under the banner of one church this would be equivalent to establishing the Kingdom of God on earth. No one could question his sincerity or the unity he aims at. Unfortunately the Muslim, also aiming at unity, thinks that the final revelation came much after Christ and that the prophet Muhammad was the last person appointed by God to bring about human fraternity. These enthusiastic bigots forget the fact that there is a distinction between the universal and the particular. The universality is the essence and the particular mood is substantiated by its existential uniqueness. One who knows the organic correlation between the universal and the particular will never attempt to make regimentations to cut everyone down to the same size for the sake of uniformity as Procrustes did.

In verses 41,42 and 45 Guru calls our attention to meditate on the true significance of the unifying and indiscernible aspect of the Absolute implied in the word "this." Here he repeats that only those who visualize the all-embracing unity of "this" know the exact rotation between the universal sameness and the individual uniqueness of each formation. Those seers alone escape the confounding confusion caused by the enigmatic juxtaposition of the universal and the particular, which comes again and again in the context of our life situation. Mankind is already one, and its search for happiness points to the same value. There is no other uniformity to be effected than what already exists. All we need is a constant remembrance of our natural unity in the universality of Being.

Verse 48

tanuvil amarnna śarīri, tante sattā-
tanuvil "atente" "titente" tennu sarvam
tanutayoziññu dhariccitunnu; sākṣā-
lanubhavaśālikaḷāmitōrkkil ārum.

The self encased in a body, in his eidetic consciousness,
understands all such as, "That is mine" and "This is mine"
bereft of body identity; on considering this
it is evident that everyone has truly experienced.

In one sense we are this body; when the breath is gone, it will be cremated or buried. Thereafter nobody would consider the person identified with it to be existing. When a person is physically alive we speak of him as black or white, or fat or thin, but all transactions come to an end when the body perishes. However, we know that we are more than a body, and further, we think of our body and mind only as instruments of some unknown entity which is working out its course using these tools in a mysterious way so as to achieve some mysterious purpose.

Even when we make sharp distinctions between one person and another we are aware of some unifying factor which pervades the life of all beings. This view is held even by ordinary people. A person speaks of "my body" or "his body." He might point at a certain woman's body and say, "She is my wife." Those who say that and those who hear it know that this reference is not to the mere physical body of a woman. In all relationships such as husband and wife, parent and child, friend and enemy, it is a non-physical entity which establishes a relationship with its counterpart in other embodied persons. People even refer to impersonal things or non-living entities as theirs, as for instance, "my house," "my book," "my honour," or "my religion." At St. Peter's Basilica, the Ramadan at the Kaabah in Mecca, or the Kumbha Mela at the Prayag in India millions of strangers come together and feel united as though only one spirit was animating all bodies, and pulsate with spiritual fervour. These are not necessarily the wise men of the highest kind of spiritual enlightenment. However, it is a fact that they do transcend all their physical limitations to experience the One which has no special name or form and which is truer than the truth of the existence of any one of them in particular.

When a person says, "I exist," he thinks of his body as proof of his existence. He knows that the animation of his life is confined within the limits of that body. When the same man says, "my wife," "my country," "my religion," and "my world," he is referring to a series of mental horizons that cover areas of interest which are not only outside his body, but can also be of such a wide range that they can be qualified as infinite. To have such an experience one need not be a great philosopher or a great saint. A man who fondly pats his cow or cuddles his dog and considers them as his belongings is consciously or unconsciously recognizing the homogeneity of his essence and that of his pets. When we consider that people all over the world have this universal experience, we can confidently say that, at least to some degree, every person experiences the Self and thereby he also transcends his physical limitations.

No man is too low or too mean to be admitted into the unifying experience of the Spirit.

Verse 49

akhilarumātmasukhattināy prayatnam
sakalavuminnu sadāpi ceytiṭunnu;
jagatiyil immatamēkamennu cinti-
ccaghamanayātakatār amarttiṭēṇam.

All beings are making effort in every way,
all the time, for the happiness of the Self;
in the world, this is the one faith;
pondering on this, without becoming subjected to sin, be controlled.

All living beings always show some conscious or unconscious activity: a worm wriggles, a dog runs around, a cat cleanses its face, an active man engages in effectual work, and a passive man tries to make his body and mind as relaxed as possible. All these can be brought under the banner of behavioural science. Even the slightest movements, such as turning the head, changing posture, coughing, sneezing or listening to a sound, are in response to some need. The need stimulates a physical response, a physiological readjustment, an attempt to fulfill a biological urge or a conscious attempt to have moral, intellectual or aesthetic appreciation of a situation. In short, all actions are motivated.

The greatest common factor in all conscious and unconscious behavioural motivation is the search for happiness. Yogis seek *kaivalyam,* Jñanis seek self-realization, Buddhists seek Nirvana, the Christian goal is salvation; these are all different names for the *summum bonum* of everybody's search. Many people do not believe in any religion, yet they too have formulated their own philosophy and scheme for collective endeavour to achieve the common happiness of mankind. Humanism and Marxism are examples of religion-like movements, yet are not recognized as religions. Guru wants us to go beyond the semantic fixation of the connotation given to the word "religion" so that we can easily grasp the common goal of mankind, which is nothing but man's search for happiness.

Right from the first verse to the forty-eighth Guru has alluded to that one Self which is immanent in everything, animate and inanimate. He has also consistently referred to the reality of the Self in terms of pure transcendence. In either case the Self is of the nature of knowledge. He made very clear to us that this knowledge can be all-embracing and unitive on the one hand, and at the same time, it can highlight the uniqueness of some specific modulation which has a meaning of its own. Transcendent knowledge in its purest state, that being one of homogeneity, is free of all discordance and hence it is identical with peace in its broadest and most profound sense. The Immanent Self, which expresses itself through multitudinous variegations, can be compared to the several colourful beams of light that radiate from the different facets of a well-cut diamond. Although each beam of light has only the momentary significance of tickling the colour vision of the spectator, that experience, which lasts only a fraction of a second, makes an absolute unit in itself, and its essential value is on a par with the unaccountable and infinite peace of the transcendent.

Life is always in a state of oscillation between these finite experiences at the physical or sensory level and the paraphysical and transcendent level. The happiness that permeates the peace of the transcendent and the wonder of the immanent are only two faces of that supreme value called *ananda.*

In the course of the discourse so far, on more than one occasion Guru has pointed out how a negative factor, like the contrasting shadow of light, can effectively cause a tragic slur in knowledge so that a person may mistake the unreal for the real, the non-existent for the existent and the pain-generating for the pleasure-giving. When this happens in an individual's life, his search for happiness becomes disoriented and his thoughts, words and deeds are likely to being misery to himself and to others. The Vedantins call this *avidya,* the Yogis call it *kleśa,* the Christians call it sin, the Buddhists call it *avijja,* and the Communists call it exploitation. Guru calls it *agham.*

Even a dog is capable of forgetting its body comforts to go a long way in being faithful to its commitment to its master. The love that links the consciousness of the dog to that of its master is a reciprocal one. That love erases all the diversities that otherwise constitute the psycho-physical frame that differentiates a man from a dog. If even an animal can transcend its body limitations to express love and concern, how much more possible it is for a man to visualize his unity with all and identify his happiness with the happiness of all! Recognition of this common happiness marks allegiance to the one religion or faith which is of all beings.

Verse 50

nilamoṭu nīratupōle kāṟṟu tīyum
veḷiyumahaṅkṛti vidyayum manassum
alakaḷumāẓiyumennu vēṇṭayellā-
vulakumuyarnnaṟivāyi māṟiṭunnu.

The ground, together with water, wind, fire and sky,
the functioning ego, right knowledge and the mind—
waves and ocean: what else is there?
All these worlds, having arisen, are changing into knowledge.

We sit, walk, work and when our limbs are tired we comfortably take our rest on the solid earth, the *terra firma*. It rains, water spatters on the roof and causes puddles on the ground. It flows as rivers to the mighty oceans which look so vast they seem shoreless. Fire sits concealed in the matchstick; rub it hard on the match box and it bursts into a flame. Fire is everywhere. It is in us as our body heat, in the stove on which we cook our food, in our lamps to give us light. It is in the clouds as electricity. It shines in the sky as the blazing sun. The far-off stars that shimmer at night are also fire. The gentle air we breathe is hardly noticed except when our nose is clogged or our lungs are weak. When the air is stirred it becomes an enjoyable breeze. When it blows hard it is the wind. At its worst it is a hurricane, a tornado. Open the door and come out. You are in the open. "The open" has no limits. In it are the neighbourhood, the far-off hills and dales, the whole world. You don't even need to come out, just open your eyes— that brings you to the outer world. All that is not inside is outside and with equal truth you could say that all that are outside are inside too.

Who experiences all this? Well, there is an "I-me-my-mine" generating consciousness which creates all these experiences. What is consciousness? That is my seeing and knowing and thinking and feeling and what not. Who causes what? Does "I" cause consciousness or does consciousness generate "I"? This is an eternal riddle of the mind. Mind! What is that? It is a fiction that is holding together all facts, like the sea generating waves. The sea is so cluttered with its waves, that we see only the waves. Philosophers and psychologists, who are the frogmen of the mind, assure us that there is a depth to our mind – a deep unconscious that is hiding beneath our perception, our thoughts and all the boiling emotions.

Ultimately, when we ponder over it, all these rise into the single phenomenon of pure knowledge: the knowledge of firmness, the knowledge of the flow, the knowledge of warmth, the knowledge of what is in and what is out – an ocean of knowledge cluttered with the knowledge of what was hitherto looked upon as "the known." The knower and the known blend in knowledge and knowledge alone triumphs over everything, enveloping everything and transforming everything into knowledge.

Verse 51

aṟivil irunnorahantayādyamuṇṭāy-
varumitinōṭoridanta vāmayayūm
varumivaraṇṭulapaññaḷ pōle māyā-
maramakhilam maṟayeppaṭarnniṭunnu.

Having existed in knowledge, an I-ness, in the beginning, emerges;
coming as a counterpart to this is a thisness;
like two vines, these spread over the tree of *māyā*,
completely concealing it.

"I am" is my most definite conscious experience. I am caught between two other entities. One is "this world" and the other is "this knowledge" which seems to have no limit or beginning or end, and in which the idea of my "I am" is only an arbitrarily delimited notion with an ever-fluctuating boundary.

To some extent I am composed of both these entities. I am partly of this physical world. As I can clearly distinguish my body from other bodies, I can say, "This is my body," "These are my senses and mind." I am also partly consciousness. Others relate to me with their consciousness and I relate to others with my consciousness. I do not know whether the consciousness that operates in all beings is the same or separate.

Who am I basically, fundamentally, truthfully? To decide this, I should know what is the reality which gives rise to the experiencing of "I" as well as "this." What am "I" absolutely, and what is "this" absolutely? Relativistically, "I" am not "you" and "this" is not "that," but that is not the ultimate truth. The search for truth is necessitated by the fact that very often our knowledge is erroneous.

Guru compares *māyā* to a tree that is overladen and concealed by two creepers called "I" and "this." The analogy of a tree is very suggestive. A tree has its roots and its ultimate fruition. Similarly, it has branches which can be schematically reduced to its two sides, the right and the left. We can make mistakes on all these four counts. The misunderstanding of the very basis of truth is an epistemological error.

The misunderstanding of the value of truth is an axiological error; this can also come as a teleological error in our pursuit of life. Our incapacity to reduce the phenomena of the sensory world to unified principles, such as one prime matter, is an ontological error. To have no normative notion with which to discern truth from falsehood and to lose our heads in fantasy or preconditioned prejudices is a methodological error. Thus, there are four basic errors.

To correct these errors, the Upaniṣads give us four great dictums. "I am the Absolute" is a dictum for correcting the fundamental or the epistemological error by which one comes to the belief that "I am this body." The dictum "This Self is the Absolute" can correct notions such as "I am happy or unhappy, sickly or strong." This dictum gives the normative notion of the Self as the measure of all things. Ultimate evidence is "Self-evidence." It enables us to avoid methodological errors. The dictum "This knowledge is the Absolute" gives a unitive understanding of the phenomenal world and thus helps us to avoid making ontological errors. In our actual life situation such knowledge prevents us from exaggerating love or hatred and help us curb desires that are likely to lead us into snares. "That you are" is the classical dictum given by every teacher, by way of instruction, as the ultimate goal to seek. The fruition of spiritual search lies in the realization of "That" as one's own Self. If one knows this, he also knows what to seek and in which direction, and thus he will not commit the teleological error of taking off on a wild goose chase.

Verse 52

dhvani mayamāy gaganam jvalikkūmannā-
laṇayumatiṅkal aśēṣa dṛsya jālam;
punar aviṭe tripuṭikku pūrttinalkuṃ-
svanavumaṭaṅṅumiṭam svayam prakāśam.

The sky will glow as radiant sound—
on that day, all visible configurations will become extinct in that;
thereafter, the sound that completes the three-petaled awareness
becomes silent and self-luminous.

We come to know many things by seeing them. All the things we see are also named and explained to us by someone or other in many words. Compared to what we have come to know through hearing and through word-content, what is otherwise known is meagre. Even a person devoid of the faculty of physical hearing is exposed to word-content. Word is structured sound. When sound is structured, it gains psycho-dynamic power. The very stuff of our world is said to be the Word. Sound is vibration. By altering the pitches and frequencies of the vibration we create words that govern our lives. We use words to hurt, to command, to instruct, to govern, to lead, to appeal, to console, to express grief, to describe, to paint visions, to tickle the soul into soaring high into the heights of sublimity and to lead the mind into great depths. Sound can shake us and also pacify us.

Sound is a quality, or the intrinsic nature of *ākaśa* – the all-filling psychic space. All things exist in the space of *ākaśa*; hence, sound can affect, influence and alter things. In verse 2, the Guru told us that this entire visible world is a modification of the light of the sun. In a higher and broader sense, the space he refers to is the firmament of consciousness. The sun that shines in the space of consciousness is knowledge.

Knowledge is compared to light. There is a range of light which varies from the most feeble flicker to the highest brilliance, brighter than the radiance of a million suns. Knowledge of things is feeble and knowledge of the Self is radiant. In this verse, Guru speaks of a state in which the space of the psyche blazes forth in great brilliance with its word dynamics.

When light increases it removes all shadows. Things are seen only by contrasting light with shadow. If all shadows are removed, the nature of visibility changes. Not only are the light and the illuminated unified into one, but the seer is also united to the seen and the act of seeing. Thereafter, only brilliance exists. In the *Māṇḍūkya* and *Chāndogya Upaniṣads* everything of the past, the present and the future is said to be the modification of *aum.* The world of the gross, the subtle and the causal are all covered by the symbolic word formula, *aum.* What remains when the secret of *aum* is revealed is the final silence into which everything seen, heard or known vanishes.

The tribasic notion of the knower, known and knowledge is unified into the still voice of the One Absolute. In that, there is neither vision nor sound. There exists only the One that shines by Itself.

Verse 53

itil ezumādima śaktiyiṅṅu kānu-
nnitu sakalam perumādī bījamākum;
matiyatil ākki marannitāte māyā-
matiyaruvān mananam tutarnnitēnam.

The primal energy implied in this
is the seed from which everything here proliferates;
having understood that, without forgetting
to clear the mind deluded by *māyā*, meditation should continue.

Māyā is a context, a situation, an appraisal or judgement which tends to be torn between the duality of acceptance and rejection, admiration and aversion. It appears to be truth and falsehood simultaneously or alternatively. Casually, two people are attracted to each other. A strong sentiment of love arises between them. They are surprised at their total acceptance and their endless capacity to surrender and do sacrifices to honour this noble sentiment that makes their hearts pulsate in unison. A spark of doubt arises, it smoulders and creates a thick fog of misunderstanding. Everything said and done in good faith and love reappears as evidence of selfishness and conceit. Cherishable memories become loathsome symbols of treachery and deceit. Thus, love begets hatred. This kind of dual situation is called *māyā.*

A man thinks that by obtaining riches and amassing wealth he can resolve all problems. When wealth comes it solves many problems of poverty, but, in turn, it also brings a thousand and one unanticipated evils. The same man wants to renounce all wealth to get a grain of peace. Thus, any number of examples, characteristic of *māyā,* are to be seen in everyday life.

For one moment, let us return to the source of our awareness and watch how it expands. Awareness expands at the recognition of names, forms, meanings of things and situations, apprehension of fear, doubt, curiosity and hundreds of other reactions, desires, associated memories, designs of action and the consequent plunge into an irresistible and compulsive action. The stream of consciousness and its accompanying behavioural activity are gushing out of a mysterious depth like a powerful fountain. We cannot dismiss the whole thing as a fictitious phenomenality.

In the previous verse we took notice of the still voice of *aum* which brings the mind to its culminating silence. When the process is regressively understood, the stage before that silence is the effect returning to the seed state of its cause. The stage before that is the withdrawal of all active forces to the subjective level of dreaming. Out-and-out manifoldness and the dual interplay of the subject and the object are only experienced in the transactional world of wakefulness. If the original cause is true, what comes out of it as effect is also true. There is only one difference: when one is transmuted into many, it assumes many kinds of dualities, such as above and below, left and right, inside and outside, big and small. The proliferation of duality is staggering. It is hard for a feeble mind to retain its sense of oneness when the manifold aspects are so intensely or acutely expressive, as pain and pleasure, elation and depression, or profound and profane. We are subjected to the tyranny of *māyā* only when the secret link with the unitive principle of the oneness of all in the only existence of the subsistent value of the Absolute is not cognized as the abiding factor in all instances of experience. This can be done only by cultivating a contemplative awareness of the one reality which is the core of everything.

Verse 54

uṇarumavasthayuṟakkil illuṟakkam
punar uṇarum poẓutum sphurikkuvīla;
anudinaminnane ṛantumādi māyā-
vanitayil ninnu puṟannu māṟiṭunnu.

In sleep the wakeful state does not exist
and when one wakes up no trace of sleep remains;
day by day, in this way, these two, having emerged
from the primal *māyā* woman, arise and alternate.

How do we distinguish a wakeful state from that of deep sleep? In the wakeful state the subject recognizes himself as "I am." This idea exists in conjunction with the idea of the extension of space occupied by bodies of different forms and names of varying significance. There is a recurring notion of the continuous passing of time and the awareness of the agency of oneself as the doer of things and the enjoyer of experiences. The details of the wakeful state, when closely examined, look enormous. All these items of awareness are covered by a blanket expression called "consciousness."

In deep sleep there is no "I." There are no bodies extended in time or space. There is no claim of doing or enjoying anything. It is as if all contents of consciousness had been completely removed from the mind. Does the mind exist in this state? No one can say. What is the state of mind if we are to presume its existence even when there is no awareness? Psychologists speak of the unconscious. If both consciousness and the unconscious belong to a single entity, what are its characteristics?

In verse 5 and 6 Guru speaks of the fluctuating modes of waking and sleeping, desiring and acting and of one's incapacity to comprehend pure beingness devoid of the flux of becoming. In verse 7 Guru suggests the possibility of remaining neutral to the waking state of being conscious of time, space, things and actions, and to the unconscious state of sleep, which is egoless, timeless and devoid of the awareness of things.

We only know the wakeful state. Although two wakeful states are interspersed with a gap of the unconscious, we can easily pick up the thread of the preceding occasion and continue our wakeful transactions in the present as if there had been no break. However, something suggests that some time elapsed between the time of going to bed and the time of getting out of bed. The quality of that time is a total forgetfulness of everything known, including time and one's own identity. Through an act of presumption we can structure the imaginary state of our unconscious.

Psychologists speak of consciousness as having within it the dichotomy of the conscious state and an unconscious state. This is the most inconceivable of all paradoxes. We can think of both black and white as colours; they are not contradictory. At their worst they are only contraries. Consciousness and the unconscious are contradictories. Upholding and validating two contradictories is called *māyā*. This is a beginningless paradox. Both colours and colourlessness semantically belong to the context of colour. In the same way both the conscious and the unconscious belong to the context of Beingness. Giving content to that beingness experientially is a challenge to the contemplative.

Verse 55

neṭiya kināvitu nidra pōle nityam
keṭumitu pōle kināvumiprakāram
keṭumati kāṇukayilla, kēvalattil
peṭuvatināl aniśam bhramicciṭunnu.

A long dream is this; like sleep, this perishes every day;
in the same way, dream also;
the perishing intelligence does not see
what belongs to aloneness, and hence is constantly confused.

Where do we draw a line between the wakeful and the dream state? If dream is a mythically structured image that can be placed between a haphazard caricature and an ingeniously fabricated short story, our wakeful consciousness is vastly interspersed with many such caricatures and mentally visualized myths and parables. What is common to both the experiences of the wakeful and of the dream is the subjective identity of the I-consciousness relating itself to time-sense, space-sense, thing-sense and a general orientation of events. The main differences between the two are the absence of perception in the dream and the contiguity of events in the wakeful. The memory of the wakeful comes handy to relate today's wakeful programme as a meaningful continuation of yesterday's and the day's before yesterday. The programming of tomorrow and the day after tomorrow can also be tabulated in today's wakeful state. Dream is chaotic and defies all the set conditional rules of the wakeful world. When we are in the dream we do not experience any lack of perception. No one feels any compunctions about having a haphazard, vulgar or lazy dream. In the present verse, the Guru treats both the wakeful and the dream as a grand dream and he contrasts it to deep sleep.

In the wakeful state we question, make critical judgements and make volitions to act. In the dream these are faked, but we do not notice the least difference between a wakeful questioning and the fake questioning of the dream. The same is also true of fake judgements and fake volitions. Both the wakeful and the dream become of no consequence in the deep sleep state. The senses, the mind, the intellect, memories and the ego are all obliterated.

In deep sleep everything disappears, but nothing is annihilated. Like the winter trees sprouting new leaves and the seeds that, after lying buried in the good earth, reappear in the lush green of spring, whatever is obliterated by deep sleep reappears in the dream and the wakeful as if it had never disappeared in the gap of deep sleep.

Narayana Guru treats the transcendent Absolute and the phenomenal existence as the two faces of the same truth. The fag end of the phenomenal existence is symbolically marked by the vanishing sound "*mmm*" of *aum*. When *aum* is articulated a long silence follows the half intoned sound "*mmm*". "M" symbolically represents the deep sleep and the causal consciousness of the phenomenal alternation between the wakeful and the dream.

The intellect, which fades out at the termination of dream, has no power to go beyond the opaque walls of deep sleep to estimate the change that comes over the consciousness. The aloneness that the Self enjoys beyond the last part of deep sleep is an eternal mystery. Recurring wakefulness and sleep turn one again and again from the aloneness of the Self and perpetuate the confusion of the phenomenal as the only reality that is experienced. The flight of the alone to the alone is thus only the privilege of the few.

Verse 56

kaṭalil eẕum tira pōle kāyamōrō-
nnuṭanuṭan ēṟiyuyarnnamarnniṭunnu;
muṭivitineṅṅitu hanta! mūlasamvit-
kaṭalil ajasravumuḷḷa karmmamatrē!

Like waves arising in the ocean,
bodies one by one suddenly arise, then merge again;
alas! Where is the end to this?
In the primal ocean of consciousness potent action is said to exist.

"The ocean and the waves" is a poetic allegory of great potential. Why should the ocean endlessly create waves? What makes it boil so restlessly? Does anything happen in the ocean? The answer to these questions can be "yes" and "no". New waves appear continuously on the surface of the ocean; hence we can say that something is always happening. In the same way, we can also say that nothing is happening, as it is always the same mass of water. The formation of the wave is only an appearance caused by the shape of the surface of the water.

It is agreed that the wave is only an appearance of the surface inundation of a watery mass. Negating the reality of the wave does not simultaneously prove the reality of the ocean. Is not the ocean just another appearance? The basic molecules of water are almost invisible. What causes those molecules does not satisfy the requirements of tangibility. An expanse of water is an abstract view with collective consent such as a fleet or a flock, and for this reason it is only a mental image. In Van Norstrand's Scientific Encyclopedia, the word "matter" is ignored as no longer valid or of any fixed operational meaning.

This brings us to the ludicrous situation of comparing a consequential fallacy to a fallacious cause and we get totally confused. If neither ocean nor wave are true, what could then be the ground of these two grand illusions? Both the Buddhists and the Vedantins declare the total situation as one that belongs to action, *karma.* Is action the action of anyone in particular? Not necessarily. Existence is action. It can be a generalized total action or multiple actions. This view does not help us to go far from the analogy of the ocean and the wave, we only shift our venue from poetry to metaphysics.

Those who argue in favour of the impenetrability of matter and the self-substantiation of things only prove that an indiscernible action produces several qualities, such as a mind that perceives and a body that is perceived, to enumerate only two out of the inconceivably vast field of *karma.* The phenomenologically and transcendentally reduced notion of the Absolute, reason and the perceptible qualities come together here in what the Guru calls the ocean of *samvit. Karma* is its only dynamics. The substantiality of the body is a product of the value synchronization of the assumed existence of valid or imaginary ideas.

Verse 57

alayarumāẕiyil uṇṭananta māyā-
kalayitu kalyayanādi kāryyamākum
salilarasādi śarīramēnti nānā-
vulakuruvāyuruvāyi ninnitunnu.

In the waveless ocean, endless traits of *māyā* remain
as potent and beginningless effects;
water's taste and so on make a configuration,
and with such embodied forms world upon world comes to be.

The ocean is not going to be absolutely placid one day, nor will our minds. Suppose that by some chance the sea is calm and non-eventful. Dip your finger in it and taste it. The water tastes saline. We are now looking at the ocean from another angle; not as the ocean with a wavy surface, but as saline water. In this verse the Guru calls our attention to this fact; *salila rasādi,* the saline taste of sea water. This is one whole unit of sensory experience. It takes us away from the idea of looking at the ocean in terms of waves and ocean. A pearl diver looks at the sea with the interest of diving into it to gather pearl oysters. Each interest makes a world. How many such possibilities are there in a single item like the ocean? It is hard to say.

The ocean of saline water is not the only ocean of our interest. When the experience of phenomenality bristles with several contradicting factors, such as love and hatred, pain and pleasure and truth and falsehood, we call it the ocean of *samsāra.* The vast expanse of consciousness, where cause and effects are only relative terms and the Absolute and the Relative are convertible ideas, this unnameable totality is looked upon as the ocean of *samvit.* When we are in a mood of reverence, feeling overwhelmed by the benign shower of grace and seeing the sharing of omnipresent benevolence everywhere, we think of the ocean of compassion. To a contemplative, who is merging in the peace of his beatitude, it is like immersing in the deep of the eternal.

Māyā is considered to be the beginningless process of becoming which causes the variegated phenomenality of names and forms and causes and effects. With this concept, it is not tenable to think of a being first, which is then followed by a becoming. The relationship between cause and effect is much the same as the relationship between the past and the present. It is in relation to this that we call what is already experienced "the past." After, or while experiencing the effect, its cause is deduced. In the world of consciousness countless are the effects that come to its surface as new possibilities of interest. When we see the wave as an effect we think of the ocean as its cause. When we taste the water and notice it is saline, we move away from the idea of waves and ocean to direct our interest to the sapidity of water. From there we may shift our interest to navigating in the sea, surfing in it, or fishing in it.

Again and again, we go to a state where all our interests in the world of effects are suspended, like we do in deep sleep. It will last only for a few hours and then we will wake again to engage in the pursuit of a thousand interests. Even death will not terminate the world of interest a person has initiated or promulgated. Where one person leaves it others will continue it.

The *Yoga Vāśiṣṭha* says that we do not know how many creators (Brahma) have gone before, or how many more will follow. One day of Brahma is equal to several billion human years. Each Brahma lives for a thousand cosmic years. Thus, cosmic time has no end. According to high pressure physicists, certain sub-atomic particles, like Pion, will take 10 particle seconds to cross the diameter of the nucleus of an atom and a particle second is 10^{23} seconds. Thus the infinitude of time is only one of the several constituents of the phenomenal process which the Guru calls *kalya*.

Verse 58

navanavaminnaleyinnu nāḻe maṟṟe-
ddivasamitiṅṅane cinta ceytiṭāte
aviraṭameṇṇiyaḷanniṭunnatellām
bhramamoru bhēdavumillaṟiññitēnam.

Do not think in ever-new terms of yesterday, today,
tomorrow or another day;
all the endless counting and measuring is due to confusion;
one should know that there is not any difference.

If you tell a story to a child, he will keep on asking, "What then?" Even when you finish the story by saying, "Finally the king died," he will again ask, "What then?" As in the child, in us too there is an irrepressible urge to live the new. We have the satisfaction of living a moment by experiencing it as the actualization of a cherished desire. In fact, the so-called moment is the process of our achievement or the failure of our attempt to achieve. If the mind is not filled with a holistic interest and the urge to act is not fully lived, dejection or boredom seeps in and creates an interlude between one main event and another main event. Time looms large as the fact of experience when such interludes bring the drag of expectation and ask the mind to wait.

Mind cannot wait endlessly for interesting things to happen, so it recalls past events which in some manner were exciting, agitating or disturbing. Another device which comes easily accessible to the mind is to fill the interlude with an interesting item such as a fantasy.

According to Indian psychologists, there are nine major moods and all shades of interest are clustered around them. They are erotics and compassion, heroics and hatred, fear and peace, humour and revulsion, and wonder. The dominant note of these moods can be seen either coming under a positive resonance with the harmony of the Absolute or tending to create disharmony. Erotics, compassion, peace, humour and wonder are in harmony with the perennial value of the Absolute, and the remaining four moods are opposed to cosmic harmony. With the combinations and permutations of these positive and negative attitudes, mind can get into processes that reflect innumerable states. Each mood or state has its own nucleus that is directly related to the value significance of the Absolute.

The highest value of the Absolute as a living experience is identical with happiness, and the normative notion for deciding its validity is the unexpending nature of the *summum bonum.* Everything belonging to the world of relativism has an origination and hence it is terminable. The value of the Absolute is coexistent with the beginningless and endless existence of the Absolute. For this reason, Narayana Guru equates imperishable happiness with the Self and the Self with the Absolute. Consequently, perceiving or experiencing happiness is the same as knowing the Self, and to know the Self is to transcend all limitations such as time and space, name and form, cause and effect and the duality of subject and object.

In the *Darśana Māla,* Narayana Guru says in his Vision One, *Adhyāropa Darśanam:*

When Self-knowledge shrinks,
Then prevails nescience fearful;
Ghost-like, taking name and form,
In most terrible fashion looms here.

Forgetfulness of the Self or the Absolute is called nescience. The feeling that a happy moment is gone or it is only about to come, indicates a rift or a chasm in Self-knowledge. Although the sun does not go anywhere, for the people dwelling on the rotating earth it looks as though it is rising, travelling in the sky and then setting. For those who know that time and space are only creations of the mind there are no limitations and there are no events. Therefore, remain Self-founded in the unexpending Beingness of the Absolute.

Verse 59

arivine vittatha ñānumillayenne-
ppiriyukil illarivum prakāśamātram
arivariyunnavan ennu rantumōrttā-
loru porulāmatil illa vādamētum.

Without knowledge I do not exist;
without me there is no knowledge; light alone is;
thus, both knowledge and knower, when contemplated,
are of one substance; there can be no doubt.

Everybody says "I know" or "I do not know." In the context of knowledge there is an "I" and "the field" in which "I" operates. Although vague, there is an inevitable demarcation drawn between the knower and the known. That which is known has already been mentioned as the measured, counted and categorized. The knower is like the eye of the known knowing itself. Hence, Śankara equates the knower to the eye, *dṛk.*

The eye, as the "seer," combines in it the quality of the light that illuminates and the quality of the eye that sees. The light of the Self reveals not only form but also name, context, meaning, relationship, the past, the present and the possible relationship that can be established with the future. If the light is withdrawn, there will be a sudden and total effacement of the conscious knower "I" and anything that is associated with the knowledge of the knower.

The eye does not see itself and the light does not reveal the light to itself. But the I-consciousness is conscious of the "I" that knows and the "I" that does not know. From this fact, it is deducible that the subject of the individual awareness is also an object of awareness. What is common to the subject matter of awareness and the object matter of awareness is an undifferentiated light.

If pure Self is an undifferentiated consciousness, why should we bother to know the difference between transcendence and immanence, pure knowledge and empirical knowledge, analytical judgement and synthetical judgement, cause and effect, and concepts and percepts?

The answer lies in a more fundamental question. "Are you convinced that there is only a non-differentiated consciousness? Can you dismiss your experience as non-existent?" If your honest answer to this is in the negative, you are remaining in a world of variegated forms and changing patterns, and you stumble on all the anomalies of the phenomena which can make you howl with exasperation, revel in the pleasure of the phantom and become tongue-tied with the enigmas that haunted the conscience of a bewildered Hamlet. When you are caught in this context, you have only two choices. One is to accept the dual validity of the knower and the known and accept the irreconcilable paradox of treating each as the by-product of the other and hit your head against the irrational wall of life's meaninglessness, variously described by the existentialists as nausea or nothingness. The other alternative is to turn away from the duet of the knower and the known, dismissing their passing show as phantasmagoria, and to give up your identity in the all-effacing Beingness, the truth of which you will never be conscious of to verify.

Verse 60

aṟivineyum mamataykkadhīnamākki-
ppaṟayumitin paramārtthamōrttiṭāte
paṟakilum apparatattvamennapōlī-
yaṟivaṟiyunnavan anyamākuvīla.

When knowledge is spoken of as subjected to the ego
without considering its ultimate truth,
even if that ultimate reality is spoken of in this way,
for one who knows, knowledge does not become other.

Man has a heritage of knowledge which is expressed through science, technology, theoretical speculations, literary expressions, formulations of mathematical, logical, semantic, moral and natural laws. It binds all people alike, irrespective of their individual preferences, tastes or factual placement in life. The underlying principle of all these expressions is the recognition of the oneness of truth. Truth is universal and cannot be monopolized by any person. However, in actual life situations, truth is a fact of individual experience. Not only does a person recognize truth, but he also acknowledges it as his personal conviction.

Experiential truth is centrally co-ordinated by the knower as a synthesis of what he gathers from his sensory data and intuitive speculation. For that reason, a person puts a circle around his I-consciousness and treats all knowledge that can be legitimately placed within it as belonging to his Self and calls it "my knowledge." By that he is virtually recognizing the existence of knowledge other than his, like that of another person or what is not known to him. Even the protagonists of great religious convictions, who claim to uphold the highest truth, label the truth they declare as their religion or their faith. Such an attitude is certainly opposed to the catholicity of truth.

The incapacity of a person to see beyond the limits of his mental horizon does not alienate the truth he perceives from the one knowledge that is streaming through all minds. The truth that is being manifested in all possible ways and which remains transcendental has no inherent cleavage, and its partial recognition by individuals does not cause any mutilations to truth as such.

In his *Arivu,* Narayana Guru says:

What is known here as This
is not other than Knowledge
when contemplated on.
As the Knowledge in This
is the same in all,
there is nothing anywhere
other than knowledge.

The transactional efficiency of knowledge is not only experienced among the members of the human species, but its general communicability is experienced by all beings.

In the Upanisads it is said that a cupful of water will reveal the prime quality of water in all the seven seas and the iron in a pair of scissors can reveal the property of the iron that is yet to be extracted from the mine. The unity of knowledge is also similar. It is essential to recognize this unity. All the values which man prizes and holds dear to him, such as love, justice and goodness, are derived from one central truth which is equally everybody's and nobody's in particular.

Verse 61

veḷi viṣayam vilasunnu vēṟuvēṟā-
yaḷaviṭumindriyamārnnu tante dharmmam
jaḷatayatiṅṅu digambarādi nāmā-
valiyoṭuyarnnaṟivāyi māṟiṭunnu.

External objects appear to be different from one another;
it is the function of the senses to posit for each a distinct dimension;
nescience rises as sets of names, like sky and so on,
and changes into knowledge.

Each moment comes with a new message and seems to say: "Enjoy me to the full " "I will shatter your dreams today." "Wait for me, it is not yet time." "See my beauty." "I am ugly, aren't you scared?" "Sit near me, I shall sing a song for you." This is how the passing moments whisper or shriek or signal to us. In these messages we hear promises, threats, cautions and alluring invitations. Each moment is reciprocally greeted or encountered by our mind and it passes judgements: "This situation is unpleasant." "That is fine." "Here is a beautiful person." "Oh, how clever you are." "This is frustrating." Thus, every passing experience is weighted, measured, compared, contrasted and evaluated with some hypothetical norm. The world of the visibles and the calculables is pluralistic.

There is a unitive way of comprehending all form within. For example, the pure vibration of energy in space and the rising symphony of sound in the ear are not two phenomena. When we are delighted by a gentle breeze, the air we breathe, the lungs that heave in respiration, the heart that pulsates, the neurons that carry the message of sensation and the soul that rejoices, all register their kinship with the one *prāṇa,* the vital energy that is both within and without. Who can say what is strictly inside or outside?

Once, an unfortunate Russian scientist said that a whole range of historical events has been governed, not by the march of dialectical materialism, but by the incidence of sunspots.

He was sent to Siberia in exile, but that did not stop the sun from spitting fire and from rocking the glandular stability of the sensitive mammals on earth. What was the crime of the Russian scientist? He saw the relatedness of things, the unbroken chain of events that range from sunspots to human cerebration.

The Guru sees a more fundamental oneness than the one recognized by the cosmologist. Wasn't it Kipling who said, "East is east and west is west, and never the twain shall meet..."? But Narayana Guru says that the easc is not the east and the west is not the west because they are notions and they only meet in the world of names. As we are in the habit of counting and contrasting all sense impressions in terms of our own preferences, we force ourselves to live in a divided world. The hard facts comprehended by the soft-ware of the mind are always spiralling upwards from the dark depth of the alpha— first as sensations, then as perceived objects, situations of love and hate or painful and pleasurable encounters— and finally, at the omega point, they vanish as mere names.

Verse 62

paravaśanāy paratattvam entetennō-
rkkarutarutennu kathippatonninālē
varumarivētu varā kathippatālē
paramapadam paricinta ceytiṭēṇam.

Do not think of the absolute truth overpowered by the sense of "mine";
what knowledge comes from merely saying "do not"?
This will not come by mouthing a phrase;
the absolute state is attained through relentless contemplation.

I want to achieve God-realization or salvation in this very life. What should I do for that? Mortification of the body is an excellent means. Like the wayside Indian yogi sitting on a seat of nails to meditate or like a Carmelite friar wearing a coarse robe, you can fast and pray and subject yourself to flogging. Have it the hard way, as they say. Another way is to beat a drum and cymbals with hysterical devotion. Sing loud and dance or walk in procession shouting the name of God. There is still another way, learn to contort your body and sit in 108 postures every day, breathing in grunts, hisses or hiccups. If you are called by God, you can distribute tracts and call on your neighbours to embarrass them or choke them with your insistence on quoting from scriptures. Lead an army of faithfuls shouting "Jehad" and kill those who refuse to accept your faith. If that sounds too heavy, go from one sacred place to another and expiate your sins by offering worship in every temple of God.

All these egotistic trips to obtain truth only harden the ego and truth will only recede like a will-o'-the-wisp. The supreme truth of the Absolute is not a thing or an entity which one can acquire by mere effort, as with riches or a position of power. It is not something that comes by piling hours upon hours of hard labour.

Okay then, let us give up and wait for salvation to come as and when it pleases. Will this attitude help? No, it will not. Left to itself, the mind will only go from one fantasy to another hungering for gratification of desires. Mere negativity will not take anyone anywhere.

How about reading the wisdom books of all realized souls or repeating religious maxims and formulae? One can become very scholarly by reading books. It may help you become a pedagogue or help you to impress others, but it will not assure you emancipation.

What is left to be done now? Adopt the attitude given in the very first verse of instruction in this series. Dim the light of the ego. Calm the mind by turning the senses inward, and discern the seeing light from the seen. Notice with reverence the same self-luminous light that shines as the nucleus of all sights, all sounds and all experiences. Know this intimate inner truth to be the same as that which is sought after and searched for as if it were a far-off reality. Know also that it is the same light that appears as the entire world. In the peace of your heart discard and recognize, constantly and without break, until the all-embracing Absolute alone shines in and through and over and above everything.

Verse 63

ar̲ivil irunnaparatvamārnnitāṭi-
yar̲ivineyiṅṅar̲iyunnatenniyē tān
paravaśanāy ar̲ivīla paṇḍitaṅ tan
parama rahasyamitāru pārttiṭunnu?

Apart from remaining in knowledge without becoming other than it
and knowing this knowledge here,
struggling in frustration, one does not know;
who sees this supreme secret of the wise man?

The act of knowing happens only in the present. Most people look upon the knowledge of the present as only a passing transaction of little worth. When we think of realization, the picture that comes to our mind is one of a future event of great consequence. We expect it to be exciting, awful and incomparable to everything. We are told that one gets it only after a hard struggle. How can the present, which is only you and I and this mundane world with its daily chores, be the ultimate reality? It cannot be. At least this is what we decide.

Let us think of the state of spiritual absorption. In this state there is no distinction between the knower and the knowledge; there is no point saying what one should know or should not know. Even though in this state knowledge prevails, it has not differentiation within it. It is neither the knowledge of anything nor of anyone. We presume it to be knowledge because we have no words with which to describe it. In deep sleep we do not know what is happening. We cannot say that either knowledge or non-knowledge prevails. There is no ego in deep sleep to either be a cognizer of the state or a director of it. In the dream state we cognize many things, but we have no power to change the course of a dream or to get into a critical examination of its content while the dream is going on. There is a definite knower in the wakeful state of here and now and he has a clear-cut knowledge. The knowledge of the waking state is of the universal and of the particular. It is of things as well as ideas. It is of the concrete as well as the subtle. We can programme and alter the activities of the present. We can make the quality of the present bright or dark, fascinating or dismal. We are not only the knowers but also the directors of the present theme of knowledge. If a dream is a fiction, the transaction of the present has the validity of the factual. In the wakeful state one can choose to react, or withdraw, critically evaluate and contemplatively reflect. It is the only state which gives us the power to direct our thoughts so as to penetrate deeply into the meanings of things.

Without altering the structural existence or the pragmatic utility of the clothes we wear, we can easily judge that the material they are made of is cotton or wool. It can be taken further to the fundamental reality of primal energy. It is only a matter of knowing. This does not tamper with the material actuality of the clothes, but the reality of the clothes will give an altogether different dimension to our knowledge. In the same way, while being in the wakeful world of transaction, one can also recognize it as the one knowledge that changes into dream, deep sleep and the state of spiritual absorption. It is always and only one knowledge. This realization can only come here and now. There is no need to be excited about it. It is a simple matter of knowing. However, this knowledge makes all the difference to the meaning of life. The knower of this knowledge in the here and now is a true seer.

Verse 64

prativiṣayam pratibandhamēṟi mēvu-
nnitine nija smṛtiyē nirākarikkū
ati viśadasmṛtiyāl atītavidyā-
nidhi teḷiyunnatinilla nītihāni.

Dismiss your memories of each object of interest,
which cause a state of obstruction;
the vast expansive memory, which can reveal
the priceless ultimate knowledge, is not unjustified.

Mind is never at rest. It is always inquisitive, wanting to know what is happening around. It looks through the windows of perception. Anything that catches its attention is immediately linked to an associated idea. Associations are not always strongly linked like cause and effect; in fact, even a remote resemblance can be more than enough to keep the mind jumping from one memory to another. Memory brings along the emotional colouration of a previous event and this is relieved, vividly sometimes, vaguely at other times and sometimes with exaggerated sentiments. Bergson speaks of it as the pulling of the thread out of a ball of yarn. It has no end. It keeps on coming and coming with bunches of forgotten events and people.

Memory has its echo in the indulgence of futuristic fantasy. When it is retrospective, it becomes regret and remorse, and when it is prospective, it becomes anxiety. On the whole memory is tied up with worries.

Pavlov exemplified the conditioning of the reflexes by his famous experiment with the dogs that salivate at the sound of a buzzer. This phenomenon of conditioning permeates the entire field of learning. In Sanskrit the storing of the memory of an impression is called *saṃskāra. Saṃskāra* means culturing or processing. An impression is processed to become a conditioned state. When a conditioned memory is further consolidated it becomes a *vāsana,* an incipient memory.

Another name for Eros is *smaran,* the one who reminds. All desires are evoked by the urge to enjoy. The urge to enjoy is like the sprout sleeping in a seed; it wakes up when conditions are favourable. The antidote to *smaran* is *smaraharan* (the burner of erotic memories), or Siva. Siva's third eye is to burn away the impulse that creates unwholesome craving. In the *Bhagavad Gita,* pure knowledge is glorified as a fire that burns away the dross of action. Memories that bring anxieties and worries should be discarded with discernment. The word, *pratibandham,* given in the original verse, is to be taken as the obstruction of the Real which is veiled by clusters of relativistic memories.

We wake up to the memories of the phenomenal because we have forgotten the original memory of our real identity. In reality we are the pure existence of absolute happiness, *sat-cit-ānanda.* If this is remembered, it will cure us from the ills of all relativistic memories.

Verse 65

orukuṟi nāmaṟ'yattatonnuminni-
lluru maṟavāl aṟivīlunarnnitellām
aṟivavar illatiraṟṟatākayālī-
yarumayeyāraṟiyunnahō! vicitram.

Nothing exists here that we have not known once;
veiled by form, all this is not wakefully known;
being boundless, there is no one who knows;
who is there to know this dear wonder? Alas! It is strange!

Knowledge as an experience is the recognition of familiar concepts structured in a certain way. In the flux of consciousness new configurations arise and for a moment they may look very unfamiliar or, as in most cases, too familiar to be specially noticed. When a sense of unfamiliarity arises it comes as a question "What is this?" "What does it mean?" "How?" "Why?" or "Which?" In search for the answer we go from the presented to what is not immediately obvious. In other words, we need to go from the effect to the cause. As we begin to probe, what appears to be unfamiliar at first will show a few factors that are known, and this is followed by a recall of the cause and effect context to which it belongs. In a systematic way, we can go from one previously known concept to another by restructuring the given situation. Consciously or unconsciously, we always do this. Tacitly everyone agrees that everything can become known, otherwise no one would bother to make any research in fields that are apparently forbidden.

The Socratic method of solving the most complex of problems by serializing questions of a very simple order exemplifies the predetermined faith that everyone knows everything. The lack of recognition is a forgetfulness of the relationship between a particular effect and its cause. A wrongly structured memory can often be a stumbling block in recognizing another unique way of structuring. This difficulty is already alluded to in the previous verse.

In Plato's Dialogue Socrates says:

> ... the Soul, since it is immortal and has been born many times, and has seen all things both here and in the other world, has learned everything that is. So we need not be surprised if it can recall the knowledge of virtue or anything else which, as we see, it once possessed. All nature is akin, and the soul has learned everything, so that when a man has recalled a single piece of knowledge – learned it in ordinary language – there is no reason why he should not find the rest, if he keeps a stout heart and does not grow weary of the search, and learning are in fact nothing but recollection.

In the present verse, Narayana Guru agrees with Socrates that what we call learning is only recollection.

Socrates gave Meno a demonstrative proof of this theory. He drew a geometrical figure of a square divided into four equal squares. He put simple questions to a slave boy to derive all the attributes of that figure. The boy first answered him smartly then came to utter confusion and perplexity. At one stage he simply gave up his attempt to solve the problem. But ultimately, when Socrates changed the mode of questioning, the boy succeeded in bringing out all apparently hidden secrets.

Knowledge can be looked at from the existential angle of its content, the ideal angle of its form and the essential angle of its significance. According to present day physics, at the subatomic level, existence and nonexistence are relative terms and nobody can predict what particle is going to change into what other particle. Thus, everything could be anything in the infinite progression of the flux of energy. All reductions and elaborations in mathematical logic are only formal restructurings of the implied idea. Essentially all formulations in consciousness should be the same at the causal level. Thus, the essential unity in the knowledge of all is undisputed.

A formally restricted entity reveals the uniqueness of one modulated value at the expense of concealing the all-inclusive Absolute, which is the ever-abiding reality of all. It is strange how we do not see the Real when we become obsessed with the actual.

Verse 66

ira mutalāyavayennumiprakāram
varuminiyum; varavaṟṟu nilpatēkam;
aṟivatu nāmatutanne maṟṟumellā-
varumatutan vaṭivārnnu ninniṭunnu.

Food and all such always come again as a matter of course;
that which remains free of becoming is one;
we are that knowledge itself; all others
also remain as its forms.

When an ant is hungry it goes in search of a thrown-away bread crumb or a dead cricket. When fledglings cry from hunger in the early dawn the parent birds leave the nest to look for worms. When a fisherman nets a big catch he can sell part of it to buy other provisions and make a saving to meet the contingency of unpredictable days. Those who live a sophisticated life with regular incomes and make their purchases from the nearby shopping centre, do not know the anguish of the little ant, the birds and the fisherman, who do not know how long they will have to toil and hang around or move around in pursuit of the prey which exists in an unpredictable range of probabilities. Even those who have the neat arrangement of a fat checkbook or bankcard and an opulent department store may at times not find the fruit or vegetable they want or a particular brand of a manufactured product. It is not hard to envisage the coming together of several uncertain and unpredictable events, which occur like favourable chances ordained by a benign God to keep the scarcity/supply ratio at an almost foreseeable pace. It is a well-known fact that most living beings get their daily food. Wild animals, like wolves for instance, which are not always lucky in getting their daily meat, are favoured by nature and are adjusted to a feast-and-fast pattern.

The daily and cyclic needs to which living beings are subjected have a harsh imperativeness. When the need is categorical, such as the intake of air, water and food, nothing is more natural than seeking its immediate fulfillment. Although the need is precipitated by a world of mechanistic determination, the fulfillment happens like the manifestation of a miracle in a rat-maze of possibilities. In some areas of the world even items of abundance, such as fresh air and drinking water, are becoming scarce. There is no promise that every need will be fulfilled. If our board and lodging on earth is hosted by a steward, nobody seems to have seen him, so all our contracts and pledges are made as ex-party decisions. On the surface of the earth, including its burrows and crevices, in the water and in the air live a multitude of beings that are in need of their daily or periodic nourishment. In spite of continuous poverty in certain countries, when we look at the proliferation, growth and longevity of the several species of beings that are earth-bound, we cannot but wonder how at least a maximum number of them are provided for daily by the unpredictable matching of probabilities, such as a smart cat succeeding in catching a partridge, while a lame cat will find sympathy in a lonely woman, or a herd of caribou escaping the pursuit of the most determined pack of wolves and the tired wolves coming upon a stray deer.

Thus, becoming is a process in which necessity enters into a dialogue with probability that again and again equalizes the balance between the need and supply with a certain amount of scarcity left behind to spur the onward movement of intentionality, which in turn becomes the substance of phenomenal existence.

In and through all these variables, there remains a constant. That is pure knowledge. In an earlier verse, Guru defined the Self as the knowledge that knows even when concealed in darkness. He is speaking here of the same knowledge which is not different from the Self.

The phenomenal becoming and the changeless pure knowledge when taken separately may look dichotomous, as in the works of Edmund Husserl and Martin Heidegger, and afterwards made unbridgeable by Jean Paul Sartre in his *Being and Nothingness.* This danger in speculative philosophy was foreseen by the Guru from the beginning and he carefully avoided the chasm by presenting the objective world of facts and the subjective world of ideas both as aspects of the one primal substance. In verse three he compares the phenomenal manifestation to the formation of waves on the surface of the watery depth of the oceanic treasury. The key word in this verse is *vaṭivu,* form. What we call the world is a formation and its never-ceasing proliferation. Although the wave is an appearance, it is an appearance substantiated by real water which has irrefutable existence, and that form can cause a heavy toll by killing a million people when it assumes the demonic dimension of a tidal wave. As Husserl rightly pleads, there is no separation between existence and absence. The Guru is not pleading here for the integration of appearance and reality, but for the recognition of the non-differentiation of the two.

The key word in the previous verse was *aruma,* the dearest of all values. We can re-apply here the analogy of the one sun with its countless beams of radiation which Guru gives in verse two. In terms of energy, the sun and the sunlight are the same. Sunlight, however, can assume the shape and colour of what it illuminates. This illuminating aspect is termed in this verse as *vaṭivārnnu ninniṭunnu.* The essential reality of all forms is the same dear value, the *aruma* of the previous verse.

Verse 67

gaṇanayil ninnu kaviññatonnu sādhā-
raṇamiva ranṭumoẓiññoranya rūpam
ninavilumillatu nidrayinkalum mē-
linanagarattilumeṅṅumilla nūnam.

One is beyond what can be counted,
the other is ordinary; other than these two there is not any other form
existing in waking, or in dream,
or in some city of the gods; this is certain.

Each day several things come to pass, many are our transactions. We are conscious of the events and the people that come into our life, of our interactions and transactions, and we are also conscious of how each of these items gives way to the next. The content of our transactional consciousness is measurable, observable, calculable, inferable, conceivable; consequently we can judge the relative merit and demerit of what we experience. Our transactional world is empirically valid.

While all these transactions are going on, we are also aware of an overall consciousness that is not separable either from the field of our transactions or from the transacting agents. What is termed here as "overall consciousness" is an inadequate term because it includes the known as well as the unknown and the conscious as well as the unconscious. We do not know where it begins or where it ends. It seems to be independent, self-founded, all-by-itself, and anything we experience, including our very selves, is part and parcel of it and entirely depending on it.

There are the two spheres of our experience, of which the former is ordinary and the latter is beyond adequate comprehension.

In the transactional world we discern the merit of things, persons and actions by using various kinds of norms or criteria. The physical world is governed by physical laws; these include the chemical, the biological and even the laws of mathematics. Those who want to transact with physical entities should learn to understand and appreciate the law that governs each field or each entity. Apart from these physical laws there are many man-made laws, conventions, taboos and social contracts, and although these are relativistic and alterable, we may have to go a long way with most of them for the sake of social harmony. When it pinches we can revolt and reconstitute the law.

The transactional world does not limit itself that way. There is room for mistaking the identities of our roles, false projections, pretentious deeds, evil motives and above all our many illusory and hallucinatory experiences. To guard against all these, science and scientific ways of disciplining our life will help to provide us with worldly wisdom. Our present day education, social welfare programmes, public health services and the judiciary are geared to meet these demands.

Man is not satisfied with all that. There is a deep need in him to seek and find the ultimate. Some people turn to their own inner consciousness and tax their brain with many hazardous disciplines in the hope of finding a reality which is other than the ordinary and different from the totality to which they belong. Some of them stumble on pet theories or strange aberrations of their nervous system and become obsessed with their queer experiences. Some others look for clues in their dreams and decide to see the ultimate face to face in visions. In the eleventh chapter of the *Bhagavad Gita,* when Arjuna asks for the vision of the Supreme, Krishna says, "See whatever you desire to see." From this it is evident that most visions are psychic projections of one's own wish fulfilment. Then there are those who think that the ultimate is not in this world but in heaven, or in another world, and a place can be secured there by doing meritorious acts in this world, or by pleasing God, or by bribing some intermediary agent. Narayana Guru dismisses all these as irrelevant attitudes and approaches.

This relativistic world of transactions and its Absolute counterpart are all there is. The Absolute is the ground, the source and the only truth to be known. It is not comparable to anything. Hence it is called Allah in the Quran; yet, immediately following the mention of Allah, two epithets of praise are usually found, the merciful and the beneficent. This is highly suggestive of the attitude one can have to one's own ground. The Absolute is treated as the adorable. Our very life on earth is to be treated as an expression, a flowering and a fruition of a value, or a graded series of values that glorify the Absolute.

Verse 68

aravavaṭākṛti pōlahanta raṇṭā-
yaṟivilumaṅgiyilum kaṭakkayālē,
orukuṟiyāryyayitiṅṅanāryyayāku-
nnorukuṟiyennuṇarēṇamūhaśāli.

Like snake-rope form,
the I-consciousness enters both knowledge and the body;
on one occasion the understanding is true, on another untrue;
thus one who can discern should understand.

If we look at our individuation from an analytical point, we find that it is constituted of a body, a mind, an ego and an intellect. When the body is animated, its sensations, its experiences of pain and pleasure and the plethora of thoughts and memories that arise commingled and that flow as a stream of consciousness can be looked upon as mind. That mind is placed on the side of the "possessor" of the body and in this verse is called *aṅgi.* This body/mind complex was described in the previous verse as the "ordinary" and what was termed there as "beyond all measure" is given here as knowledge, *aṟivu.* Although this supreme knowledge, which is identical to the Self and the Absolute, is beyond the reach of mind and words, it is accessible to the intellect. The *Bhagavad Gita* (chapter VI, verse 21) says:

> That which cognizes the ultimate limit of happiness, which can be grasped by reason and goes beyond the senses, and wherein also established, there is no more swerving from the true principle.

A yogi who identifies his Self with the unalloyed bliss of the transcendental being and whose intellect is freed from the taints of the senses and mind remains stable in his inner happiness. The figure overleaf shows the approximation of the scheme implied in this verse.

Without the body there cannot be an individual, and without the mind the body does not function. According to the physiological psychologists and the neurophysiologists, mind is an epiphenomenon

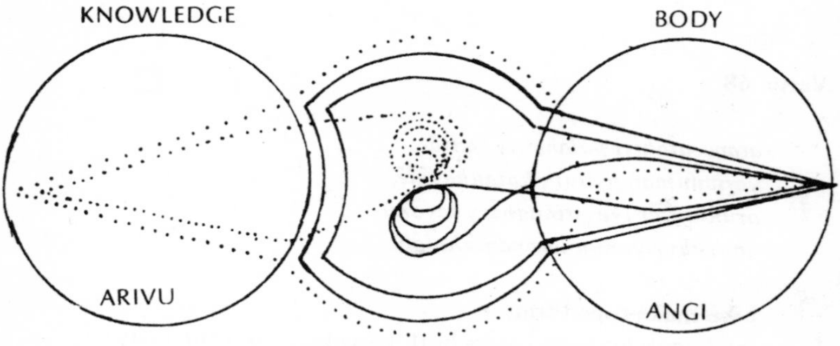

produced by the complex effect of highly organized bodily functions, such as the sensory system, the motor functions and the intensive molecular activities of the brain. So it is hard to say whether the mind monitors the body or the body monitors the mind.

A body, with its animation called mind, will only vegetate if its individuation is not consciously felt and directed by the personal identity of an ego. All goal-oriented actions are motivated and carried out by the ego. Experiences such as heat and cold, pain and pleasure, success and failure, and praise and shame intensify the ego identity.

According to the present verse, the primary interest of the ego can alternate and change the sense of belongingness of the I-consciousness. For a while it can be one with the body identity and can crave the pleasures of the senses or look for the gratification of several latent desires. Sooner or later, however, it reaches a saturation point and flings itself in the opposite direction where it identifies itself with the unknown, the transcendent, which in this verse is called knowledge.

The ego, the mind, the senses and the body have no light of their own. The only conductor of the illuminating reason of the Self is the intellect. So the ego must hire the services of the intellect to carry out the actualization of its motives in the transactional world. When intellect. So the ego must hire the services of the intellect to carry out the actualization of its motives in the transactional world. When intellect operates as a tool of the ego, the mind takes an upper hand and colours the intellect with all its pre-conditionings of love and hate, pain and pleasure and all attraction/repulsion dualities. As reason truly belongs to the Self, it occasionally jerks away from the clutch of ego to return to its own natural habitat, described here as knowledge. This automatically also turns the ego to the Self.

The ego is like a shadow. Sometimes it resembles the shadow of the Self, and at other times of the embodied finite person. It is like a form which alternately looks like a rope and then like a snake.

Guru's suggestion here is not to become fully identified with any one of these alternatives. So long as the body persists, the alternation is inevitable. What he teaches is how to raise one's consciousness above these alternations and remain in neutral zero witnessing the ceaseless sport.

Verse 69

śruti mutalām turagam toṭuttorātma-
pratimayeẓum karaṇapravīṇan āḷum
rati rathamēriyahanta ramya rūpam-
prati puṟamē perumāṟiṭunnajasram.

Hearing and such as horses yoked,
occupied by the self-image, the dexterous psychic dynamism drives
the chariot of *rati*; mounted therein, the ego
is continuously chasing each pleasing form outside.

Sweet sounds attract the ear. They are the microwaves that form the warp and woof of music. In Sanskrit, microwaves are called *śruti*. Sound is said to be the quality of ether. We are not speaking here of the medium of sound, but of the element of which it is a quality. After the failure of the Michelson-Morley experiment, scientists came to the conclusion that there is no ether. They may be right. This does not cause any despair to the Vedantin however, except for the fact that *ākaśa* is wrongly translated as "ether." If *ākaśa* is not matter, it must be non matter, or spirit. In the present context, we may understand it as an entity which can function both as a thing and as knowledge. In any case, it is good to commence a study of life from *ākaśa,* which is both thing and no-thing.

From the subtlest ether to the grossest form of matter, such as earth, there are several grades of materiality. It is well known that all physical things exist within an electro-magnetic field that is not seen; we know it only from its effect. In Guru's analogy, he begins with *śruti* (microwaves), which is close to this subtle force. Man is a bundle of nerves and nothing affects him more intensely than the quality of the sound he hears. It can lull him to sleep, rouse him to erotics, excite him to flight, or drive him mad. Although the sound we hear is caused by a vibration that disturbs the fluid in the cochlea, this is only a minor function of this organ when we consider the fact that our bodily balance to stand erect and walk on two legs depends very much on the sound functioning of this organ. Thus, the primacy given to the sense of hearing is very appropriate.

In Guru's analogy, the ego is mounted on the chariot of *rati* (the libido), which is drawn by horses (the senses, such as hearing etc.). There are two implied secrets in the analogy of the horses. One is that the horses always proceed to a goal, as our life, yoked to the senses, is always goal-oriented. Secondly, the power of locomotion is measured in terms of horsepower. This implies that the senses are capable of arousing and releasing the energy required for the motivational pursuit of life.

The reference to "hearing" in this verse is similar to the reference to beauty in verse 8. From this it is evident that each sense has its attraction and they are all equally irresistible. Although the metaphor of the chariot appears in the Gita and several Upaniṣads, the one presented here is more complex than any given elsewhere.

There are three occupants of the chariot: the self-image, the ego and the psychic dynamism. Of these, the actual execution of the driving of the chariot is assigned to the psychic dynamism, which itself is an entity constituted of four factors: the interrogating mind, the recalling memory, the judging intellect and the affective ego. The separate mention of the ego is to highlight one aspect of the psychic dynamism, but, in fact, the ego can be bracketed with the psychic dynamism, which in this verse is further qualified as dexterous.

The ego is both an existential thrust and an ontologic awareness. The awareness is perpetuated by repeatedly recognizing the identification of the knower, the doer and the enjoyer as I-consciousness, and by constantly saying "I," "me," "my" and "mine." The self-awareness of the ego is a mirroring of the eternal light of the Self. In other words, the ego is a superimposition on the Self. Although the Self is universal, indivisible, partless and formless, the superimposed ego is strongly coloured by the finitude of the body in which it functions. The self-image demarcated by the ego naturally casts a boundary line in the light of the Self. The individuation thus formed is recognized here as the image of the Self, *ātma pratima*. Thus, it becomes imperative for the ego to be flanked on one side by the self-image and on the other by the psychic dynamism, which is referred to in this verse as *karaṇam*.

From the Sanskrit term it is evident that the ego (*ahanta*) is wielding both the motivation and the instrument of pursuit. The motivation is happiness. This has a double significance. For the ego to become aware of itself the only light comes from the Self, which, by nature, is *ānanda*.

Hence, it is obviously only natural for the ego to remain wedded to happiness. The ego, however, is not a finite version of the Self, as its substance comes from *prakṛti,* which is constituted of the five elements and the three qualities known as *sattva, rajas* and *tamas.* These, while being dynamic, are devoid of any light of their own to be conscious of their functions. The ego is the only link between the Self and nature. The innate qualities of Self, mirrored by the ego, become subjected to the veiling principle of *māyā* and, as a result, confusion arises. *Ānanda* mirrored in *prakṛti* is called *rati.* The chariot is not real, but a phantom created by the image of the pleasure-giving on the constantly changing facade of *sattva, rajas* and *tamas. Sattva, rajas* and *tamas* are only principles and they have no content except in relation with the manifested elements of ether, air, fire, water and earth – or the psychic dynamism – when they have manifested through the individuation of a person.

This gives a clear picture of the ego which, goaded to seek happiness by its primary nature (the Self), finds only the confusion caused by its association with *prakṛti* when its happiness is sought in the shadowy world of the psycho-physical objects of the senses. This is certainly a most deplorable state.

Verse 70

oru rati tanneyahantayindriyāntah-
karaṇakaḷēbaramennitokkeyāyi
viriyumitinnu virāmamennu vēṟā-
maṟivavan ennaṟivōḷamōrttiṭēṇam.

One *rati* alone is expanding into the ego, the senses,
the mind, the body and all that is;
where is an end to this?
Not until one knows that he is different, none other than knowledge; remember!

According to Greek legends, there are three fundamentals: Earth, Chaos and Eros. In Indian legends, *kama* (Eros) is coupled with *rati*. *Rati* is the libidinal enjoyment of erotics. A creation myth is given in the fourth section of the first chapter of the *Bṛhadāraṇyaka Upaniṣad*. According to it, the first person that came into being was unhappy being alone. This being, longing for a mate, grew to the size of a man and a woman in embrace and then split into two. Of the two, one half became the husband and the other the wife. Fearing the guilt of incest, the woman disappeared and the entire space became filled with the man's fascination for the woman. The woman changed into the female form of every species on earth and the man mated with her by becoming a male member of all corresponding species. *Rati* is the propelling force which activates the ego into finding its gratification.

Sigmund Freud borrowed from Moll (1898) the term "libido" to describe the dynamic manifestation of sexuality. At first he thought there was a separation between ego instincts and sexual instincts. In his libido theory he says:

> What is described as the sexual instinct turns out to be of a highly composite nature and is liable to disintegrate once more into its component instincts. Each component instinct is unalterably characterized by its **source**, that is, by the region or zone of the body from which its excitation is derived. Each has furthermore as distinguishable

> features an **object** and an **aim**. The aim is always discharge accompanied by satisfaction, but it is capable of being changed from activity to passivity. The object is less closely attached to the instinct than was at first supposed; it is easily exchanged for another one, and moreover, an instinct which had an external object can be turned round upon the subject's own self...The most important vicissitude which an instinct can undergo seems to be **sublimation**; here both object and aim are changed so that what was originally a sexual instinct finds satisfaction in some achievement which is no longer sexual but has a higher social or ethical valuation.*

He further adds:

> The ego is to be regarded as a great reservoir of libido from which libido is sent out **to** objects and which is always ready to absorb libido following back **from** objects. Thus the instincts of self-preservation were also of a libidinal nature. Clinical experience had made us familiar with people who behaved in a striking fashion as though they were in love with themselves and this perversion had been given the name of **narcissism.****

In the *Bṛhadāraṇyaka Upaniṣad,* what Freud considers to be a perversion is extolled as the only true love. No one loves anything more dearly than one's own self. When the self is wrongly identified with the ego, it projects the love for the self either on external objects of the senses or on fantasies of the mind. Freud cannot see any end to this unquenchable zest of the pleasure principle. Narayana Guru asks, "Where is an end to this?" He sees one possible termination, and this happens when the knower knows that he is not different from the one knowledge of which everything phenomenally apparent is only a transient shadow.

* Sigmund Freud, *Collected Papers,* Vol. V, pp.132-33.

** *Ibid.*

Verse 71

savanamozinnu samatvamārnnu nilpī-
lavaniyil ārumanādi līlayatrē;
aviralamākumitākavēyarinnā-
lavanatirarra sukham bhaviccitunnu.

No one in this world remains free from becoming,
in a state of sameness; this is said to be a beginningless play;
to him who knows this, which is unlimited, as a whole,
boundless happiness comes.

Our life on earth is described in the Bhagavad Gita as that which is not known at its beginning, not known in the middle and also not known at its end. There are so many theories about time, but what is relevant to us is what we experience here and now. The sequential experiencing that goes on from the past to the future or from the future to the past is called becoming. In this verse the term used is *savanam*, the birth of events. Something is always being born and something is always disappearing from our attention.

The *Bṛhadāraṇyaka Upaniṣad* speaks of three aspects of life: the speech, the mind, and the *prāṇa*. The speech is that which is known, the mind is that which desires to know and the *prāṇa* is the unknown. The mind has a central place between the known and the unknown, and also between the world of external stimuli and the inner impulses. Without mind nothing is known. We need the mind for the articulation of speech and the interpretation or the discerning of the meaning of whatever is heard or experienced. Knowledge is identical with mentation. Although the mind depends on the *prāṇa*, the vital forces, it has no knowledge of its autonomic functions. In the *Chandogya Upaniṣad*, *vyāna* is adored as the vital force that fuses the *prāṇa* into *apāna* and thus helps the continuous articulation of words without needing to take special time to breathe. Thus, *prāṇa* is causally related both to the mind and also to speech. From the unknown comes that which is desired to be known and that which is known.

The world of becoming is so fabricated that only a small fragment is ever revealed to our knowledge. Human interest is also shifting from one gestalt to another. This fragment can be joyous, dreadful or painful. Two remedies are recommended in this verse for transcending the consequences of suffering. One is to know the cosmic phenomenon to be a beginningless sport and the other is to know the phenomenality itself in its entirety. What is involved in the eternal sport is the non-Self. The total knowledge suggested in this verse is the knowledge of the Self. The painful duality comes in between the experiencing of "I am" and what is "other than me." In the opening paragraphs of Sankara's commentary on *Brahma Sutra,* he presents the mistaken identity of the Self with the non-Self and the non-Self with the Self, and he considers that to be the basic ignorance that causes all experiences of misery. In our day to day experiences, our mind is veiled by a cloud of unknowing and hence our knowledge is bound to be relativistic and partial. The scriptures of all religions and all teachers or masters try to remove this screen from our minds. We are using words, which have the power to make things known to us, to throw light on what we desire with our mind and what may assail us from the unknown.

It is not easy to know everything in one comprehensive truth, but we can look at life as a sport. Take sports like football, as it is played in the United States, or boxing, they are dangerous and masochistic, yet that does not stop people from enjoying them. If a man punches another's nose outside a sport arena, this is viewed as a crime and the police may even be called. This is the difference between seriousness and a sportive attitude. In a motor race cars overturn and burst into flames, in a flying display aircrafts crash and people die. This is treated as part of the game. Treating at least part of our life as a game is well known to us, but this attitude is to be extrapolated into other areas also. No one sues a friend for libel, even when the friend publicly ridicules him before others. The sportive spirit elevates our vision and keeps us cool. In *Memories, Dreams and Reflections,* Jung mentions how he brought epileptic fits upon himself so as to attract attention. There are neurotic and psychotic traits that people do not want to be rid of.

Is poverty a sport? There are people who have taken vows of poverty. Jalaluddin Rumi says, "Poverty is my pride and obscurity is my refuge." It is all a matter of attitude. The poorest of the poor can do things which even the very richest cannot do. Permanent arrangements to feed and clothe pilgrims going to Badrinath in the Himalayas, shelters, roads and bridges all the way from Rishikesh to Badrinath or Gangotri were all accomplished by a renunciate who had nothing but a blanket as his sole possession.

Now let us pass on to the knowledge of the Self. By pushing the attitude of sport to another degree, you become the neutral witness of all. All the paradoxes we experience, such as light and darkness and love and strife, look like contradictions that cannot co-exist. In reality, however, they are enigmatically polarized and they operate like the two sides of the same coin. When we admit the dualities as aspects of the same reality, our acceptance becomes unitive. Unitive understanding leaves nothing outside. This brings peace and removes all sense of fear and misery. Total knowledge brings an all-absorbing silence. One can live in that silence even when the ear hears the tumult of the physical world and the eyes see many passing shows.

Verse 72

kriyayorukūṟitavidya; kēvalam ci-
nmayi maṟukūṟitu vidya; māyayālē
niyatamitiṅṅane nilkkilum piriññā-
dvaya para bhāvana turyyamēkiṭunnu.

Now there is action, which is ignorance,
and again there is pure consciousness, which is knowledge;
although these two are thus ordained by *māyā* to stand divided,
a non-dual vision of the Absolute brings about *turīya.*

In verses 69 and 70 the Guru called our attention to the libidinal force which is at the root of intentionality, and in verse 71 he gave us an overall picture of becoming. He made it clear that no one can escape the flux of becoming. In the present verse Guru refers to an alternating process, an ambivalent principle instituted by *māyā. Māyā* is that which is not. Hence the predicate "instituted" is to be taken only allegorically. This paradoxical alternation of interests and the knowledge of the associated contexts to which these interests belong should be understood as *māyā.*

Māyā is a wonder. The Absolute is also a wonder Wonder comprises delightful surprises as well as unexpected strokes of tragedy. When we take interest in a specific object or event we project our happiness or misery as a condition intrinsically associated with external objects or happenings. This is erroneous; yet, in the course of a day we indulge in such projections hundreds of times. At the same time all our value judgements are made on the basis of our intuitive perception of the three basic aspects of our Self, such as its existence, its self-luminous awareness and its ever-blissful state. Then, even to make an erroneous judgement, we have to borrow the light of our self. It is like a man who uses his knowledge of truth to tell a lie. Deriving pleasure from objects of interest or suffering pain and misery because of physical identification is termed here *avidya.* Comprehending the nature of the self, at least momentarily and indirectly is called *vidya.*

The occasion for this ambivalent alternation is one of action. Action is necessiated by the individual's dissatisfaction with his present state and the search for novelty, for a new state of being, or for another arrangement of his life situation which might be more interesting. This pursuit of happiness was alluded to in verse 69 as the libidinal urge. It can be directed toward objects outside or toward the self. The feverish search for happiness implies two mistakes: one is that the individual underrates the true nature of the Self because he identifies himself with a body which is given a certain name and which is considered to be one of the many things of this world. The other mistake is to think that one's happiness is conditional to a factor outside oneself. Transactionally, this identity is quite valid; it is erroneous only when we consider the basic nature of the Self. In an absolutist sense we do not lack anything, we are the very existence, knowledge and happiness that we are seeking. This identity is veiled by ignorance and this kind of ignorance is called *āvaraṇa.* The veil is not merely blank ignorance, it functions as a projection that is capable of affecting the mind with pain and pleasure. When a film is projected on a blank screen, the original white screen is veiled by the dark patches that come from the projector. Apart from this veiling, the dark patches and the shades of light appear as intriguing figures which have the power to produce a series of meaningful ensembles to the onlooker. A projection superimposed on something else is called *vikṣepa. Māyā* operates by interlacing the veiling and the projection.

When a man is in a theatre, excited by either a humorous sequence or a blood-chilling scene, he laughs or cries. After leaving the theatre, he will laugh at the folly of allowing mere shadows projected on a screen to affect him. In life we also take many things seriously and suffer. Later we may think of the same things as silly.

If a person is content and happy here and now and can transcend both *vidya* and *avidya,* he is blessed with a non-dual vision. When a person loves another person with great intensity, he or she experiences a transpersonal identity. Everybody experiences this going beyond the bodily limit to be at one with another's interest. If this possibility is widened in its scope, the limitations of name and form can be transcended. A total transcendence of the transactional experience can bring a hitherto unknown reality of our own basic nature.

There are three areas to look into: one is the transactional world of all dualities; the second one is the world of the contemplative where all forms, names and events are reduced to a single universal; and the third one is the neutral ground of the realized ones who treat both the transactional and the transcendental as aspects of one and the same reality. The *turīya,* the fourth state of consciousness referred to in this verse, is to be understood in terms of AUM, as it is described in the *Māṇḍūkya Upaniṣad.* In the transactional world we experience inevitable pains and pleasures which are characteristic of the agitations of the nervous system. There is no solution to this. It must be accepted as a fact of life. Most of our pains and pleasures, however, are imagined. It is up to us to give up all the fanciful imaginings that we generate. The ground of our transactional experiences and subjective experiences is the unmodulated pure consciousness. This can be compared to the silence that precedes and follows the articulation of AUM. "A" indicates a sudden break from silence into a world of objectivity. The known and the knower emerge with a clear distinction between them. The sound "U" indicates a gradual merging of sound into the silence from which it blared forth. Like that, in the subjective reflection, mind merges once again with the universal. "M" indicates the total extinction of the articulated sound and it symbolizes the disappearance of the duality between the knower and the known. The silence that follows brings us back to the ground from which everything started. A true knower has a transparency of unitive vision and always sees this unchanging ground of pure silence as a backdrop to all events in the flux of becoming. His intellect remains stable, steadied by this unflagging vision. This is called *sahaja samādhi,* the natural absorption of the enlightened seer. In this verse *turīya* is to be understood in that sense.

Verse 73

oru poruḷiṅkal anēkamuṇṭanēkam
poruḷil orartthavumenna buddhiyālē
aṟivil aṭaṅṅumabhēdamāy itellā-
varumaṟivīlati gōpanīyamākum.

In one substance there are many,
and in many things there is one meaning; reasoning thus,
everything becomes inseparably inclusive in knowledge;
not all know this great secret.

we live in a situation of one and the many. When you become self-conscious you feel like one placed in the midst of many. The many may look strange and even scary. When you are in a new environment the consciousness of the other is very intense. In such a context you instinctively want to defend yourself and you may either want to withdraw into your own shell or look for emergency exits from which to flee in case a contingency arises. In a strange environment you will look for a sign of friendship, such as a greeting smile, an outstretched hand to receive you and a kind word of inquiry. When this happens you brighten up and try to establish a bond with the person who symbolizes the good will of the new environment or the society to which you are a stranger. Spontaneously there manifests a bridge between hearts to reciprocate friendship. You don't need to hang on to your "I" and call the other person "you." You can now bracket yourself with the other and say "we." If in this new environment your new friend introduces you to ten others who are his friends, the love and confidence he kindles and nourishes will flow toward all the other ten. Thus you now have a bigger circle of familiar social space to own as "ours." How does this transformation come to you and to the people involved with you? To answer this question we must look into the meaning of whatever we have experienced.

Let us now take another situation. You are not in a strange place, but in a cosy room of your own secure home. You have no problems with your neighbours or any member of your family. You are left to yourself. In such a situation everything other than you seems to blend into one single harmonious whole. In the middle of this passive infinity you sit smoldering as if the person within you had split into many entities, each with a different voice and no common interest to bind them together. In this case, the one has changed into many. The solid "I" has dissipated into many fragments, like a crowd of heterogenous elements, which you want to reunite into a solid "I." Thus the problem of one and the many can arise in so many ways. Philosophers of all times have given their best attention to this.

In Plato's *Republic,* Socrates speaks to Glaucon of the one in the many and the many in the one as follows:

> We predicate 'to be' of many beautiful things and many good things, saying of them severally that they *are* and so define them in our speech: And again, we speak of a self – beautiful and of a good that is only and merely good, and so, in the case of all the things that we then posited as many, we turn about and posit each as a single idea or aspect, assuming it to be a unity and call it that which each really is.*

Again, in the dialogue with Parmenides, Parmenides calls Socrates' attention to the many that partake in the one:

> I accept that, said Socrates, and I have no doubt it is as you say. But tell me this. Do you not recognize that there exists, just by itself, a form of likeness and again another contrary form, unlikeness itself, and that of these two forms you and I and all the things we speak of as 'many' come to partake? Also, that things which come to partake of likeness come to be alike in that respect and just insofar as they do come to partake of it, and those that come to partake of unlikeness come to be unlike, while those which come to partake of both come to be both? Even if all things come to partake of both, contrary as they are, and by having a share in both are at once like and unlike one another, what is there surprising in that? If one could point to things which are simply 'alike' or 'unlike' proving to be unlike or alike, that no doubt would be a portent, but when things which have a share in both are shown to have both characters, I see nothing strange in that, Zeno, nor yet in a proof that all things are

* Plato, *The Collected Dialogues,* Bollingen, 1973, p. 742.

> one by having a share in unity and at the same time many by sharing in plurality. But if anyone can prove that what is simply unity itself is many or that plurality itself is one, then I shall begin to be surprised.*

In chapter IX of the *Bhagavad Gita,* Kṛṣṇa says:

> Always singing praises of Me, ever striving, firm in vows and saluting Me devotedly, they are ever-united in worshipful attendance;
>
> Others also, sacrificing with the wisdom-sacrifice, unitively, dualistically, as also in many ways facing universally everywhere, worshipfully attended on Me.

All shades of value appreciation, ranging from the most negative, such as boredom, frustration, intense physical pain or mental agony, to a neutral state of evenness of mind and to the highest form of bliss or ecstasy, come in one single scale of gradation which is called *ānanda.* This value appreciation is called *arttha. Artha* means wealth and meaning. Wealth is meaningful only when its appropriate use becomes relevant to a situation. An appropriate meaning depends on many factors, such as time, space, and interrelationship between things. The problem of one and the many is most relevant in discerning the many.

We look for values such as good health, sound mind, command of language, dexterity of action and power to assert and accomplish. These and many other values can come like spokes in a wheel and be united in one and the same person. All these become appropriate values only if their union within the individual makes him happy.

In the present verse, the Guru speaks of the one meaning in the many things and the many meanings in one thing. To live this unity with a full appreciation of all the varieties of differences that constitute any life situation, a discipline that can continually harmonize all pairs of opposites is needed. Music is a good example of striking harmony.

Narayana Guru visualizes an inseparable inclusiveness, in which the one and the many can be harmonized. When a person attains this unity he recognizes the one fatherhood of God, the one motherhood of nature, the one brotherhood of all sentient beings and the whole world as his country.

* *Ibid.*, p. 923.

Verse 74

poṭiyoru bhūvil asankhyamappotikkuḷ-
ppeṭumoru bhūvitinilla bhinnabhāvam;
jaḍamamarunnatu pōle cittilum ci-
ttuṭaliluminnitinālitōrkkil ēkam.

Innumerable particles of dust inhere in earth,
and there is no difference in the earth that constitutes the particles;
just as inert matter exists in consciousness, consciousness finds its expression
here in the body; therefore, when contemplated, this is one.

The relation between a particle of dust and the whole earth symbolizes the relation between our peripheral life and its infinite basis. At the surface level, our senses and mind are encountered by many specific entities and each such encounter changes into a miniature world as, fully or partially, it occupies our interest for the time being. Each such world can be compared to a particle of dust. Every particle has its rightful place in the whole. Similarly, even a triviality has its niche in the general edifice of life.

In its sensual or social pursuits, mind comes to a satiation point, or a point of boredom or frustration, and it recoils again and again to its own depth in search of the meaning or worth of life. This is the returning from the dust to the universal ground. Great masters, who were well established in this ground, such as Vasiṣṭa, Vālmīki, Vyāsa, Buddha, Yājñavalkya, Christ, Muhammad and Narayana Guru, relied entirely on the free flow of wisdom that came from the one common ground of all to which they gave different names, such as Paramātman, Narayana, Puruṣottama, Tattatah, Ātman or Brahman, God, Allah and Aṟivu or knowledge. All were fully conversant with the Absolute, its attributes and the innumerable modes that come into manifestation and disappear on the surface of consciousness.

When the mind is identified with the attributes of the modes it has little chance to be conversant with the ground. Like the root that nourishes a tree, the light of the Absolute arises out of the ocean of the unconscious as a blazing island of pure resplendence, life sap flows into the veins like the sweet elixir of immortality, mind's inertial sloth changes into the jubilation of inspired visions and the woes of a lifetime disappear like a mist in the flood of sunlight. Such moments of blessedness are lived by everyone at least for a short period of time. This is a recurring experience for poets, musicians. artists and contemplatives.

It is part of the physical condition that its modes fall into harmony, become imbalanced and jolted, and go into periodic states of inertia. This aspect of nature's phenomenality has full sway over the world of finitude, the world of dust. The modes and their attributes, being part of the extension and the illumination of the primordial substance, come into union again and again with their own ground. Religious seekers of truth think of this favour as a divine grace and remove all the egoistic obstructions of the conscious self to receive this communion which comes from within. Jesus Christ describes this as brides who, burning their midnight lamps, keep their vigil for the arrival of the unpredictable Beloved. The mystic lives in the nuptial chamber of his divine Beloved and in this union the duality of the speck of dust and the universal ground is abolished.

Verse 75

prakṛti jalam tanu phēnamāẓiyātmā-
vahamahamennalayunnatūrmmi jālam
akamalar ārnnaṟivokke muttu, tān tān
nukaruvatāmamṛtāyatiṅṅu nūnam.

Nature is water, the body is form, the Self is the depth;
"I am, I am" – thus, a restless repetition like a series of waves;
every inner blossom of knowledge attained is a pearl;
indeed, whatever each finds delight in is the nectar of immortal bliss.

In the transactional world direct perception gives valid knowledge. To ascertain its truth we do not need to go to another authority. We cannot see God or the Absolute or the Self. When it comes to such matters, which are subjective, we need assurances and guidance from others. It is in this context that *a priori* wisdom teaching becomes an absolute necessity. To pass wisdom from one who has experienced to another who has not word-testimony is used. In word-testimony what comes most handy is analogy. The Buddha, Jesus Christ and Sri Ramakrishna used parables and allegories to teach their disciples. One of Narayana Guru's favourite analogies is the ocean.

The ocean is the favourite theme of artists, poets, novelists, story-writers, philosophers and mystics. Maxim Gorky's *Song of the Stormy Petrel,* Victor Hugo's *Toilers of the Sea,* and Samuel Taylor Coleridge's *Ancient Mariner* aptly describe the ferocity of the sea. Vedantins compare the dreadful aspect of the sea to the miseries of the world when they use the expression *bhava sāgara.* In this verse Narayana Guru uses the analogy of the sea to illustrate the relationship of man with the Absolute and also the values which man relates himself to. In this context his reference is to a sea of knowledge, *samvit sāgara.*

There is nothing so beautiful and fascinating as sitting on the soft white sand of a peaceful beach watching a gentle ocean on a moonlit night. Silver-crested waves come rhythmically to cast long rows of pearl-like foam upon the sand. Every bubble of the foam glitters in the moonlight and mirrors the moon, the starry heavens and the dark world. After a moment the bubbles burst and disappear. In a little while another wave deposits fresh foam upon the sand, new bubbles to shimmer, burst and disappear. This game goes on and on, endlessly.

One wave followed by another shows the sequence of time. A wave gathering momentum, making undulations on the surface, rolling and beating against the shore reveals the contents of a unit of time. The fact that the ocean was there before any living creature appeared on earth and that it will continue to be even after all creatures will have perished suggests the eternity of time.

In this verse the Guru compares the water of the ocean to nature. Water is a principle like nature. It manifests itself in many forms: as the lake, the clouds, the snow, the moisture in the atmosphere, the fluids in a living body and the sap in vegetative life. Our bodies are compared to the foam. Like the little bubbles of foam, the body lasts only for a little while and while it exists it is animated by consciousness, mirroring a world of light and darkness. With the bursting of the bubble the world is also gone.

The restless waves that come one after another are compared to the recurring consciousness, "I am, I am." There is anguish and dismay when the ego is vainly chasing shadows. If the same I-consciousness turns inward, it becomes honey-filled flowers of inner awareness. The ocean is likened to the Self. The depth of the ocean is proverbially unfathomable and so is the Self. In verse three the Self was compared to a treasury of watery depth. In the present verse Narayana Guru refers to the pearls of knowledge that gladden the heart of the seeker of wisdom. In every item of joy that gladdens the soul the Guru sees the relishing of the elixir of immortality.

Verse 76

maṇal aḷavaṟṟu coriñña vāpiyinmē-
laṇiyaṇiyay alavīśiṭunnavaṇṇam
anṛta parampara vīśiyantarātmā-
vineyakamē bahurūpamākkiṭunnu.

As countless grains of sand ceaselessly blown onto
the surface of a pond generate ripple after ripple,
by untruths successively blown,
the inner self is transformed from within into various forms.

We think that our inner self is a private possession secretly guarded in the confinement of our heart. In fact, nothing is more exposed to the caprices of the outside world than our sensitive inner self. In this verse the Guru compares our inner self to a neglected pond in the middle of a wasteland where sand storms are common. The wind blows, continuously whipping up sand from all sides to disturb the tranquil limpid water. Several patterns of ripples arise on the water's surface and distort all the reflected images. Further, the same sand, after polluting the water by making it murky, sinks to the bottom and changes the formation of the terrain. Thus, continuous affectation comes to the terrain, to the water and to the surface; or in other words, to the ground, the content and the mode.

The sand storms to which we are exposed are the many phenomenal items that come to us as the perceptual images of what we see and the conceptual images of the words we hear or read. Everything we see, touch, smell, taste and hear affects our consciousness and causes reactions of love, hatred or indifference. Consequently, we experience pulls of attraction or repulsion. These correspond to the everchanging checkered patterns the ripples make on the surface of the pond. The murkiness of the water corresponds to our changing moods and the mud that settles on the bottom, altering the pattern of the terrain with deposits of one layer, upon another, is the conditioning. This in Sanskrit is called *saṁskāra.* The *saṁskāra* of a previous life, or the innate disposition with which we are born, is called *vāsana. Vāsana* itself is a superimposition of ignorance on the Self.

Rousseau says that when seeds germinate their shoots grow vertically. Later, horizontal winds blow and bend their stems, making them grow into crooked trees, or force creepers to entwine up on them. In our social life we are exposed to the horizontal pressures of society and that distorts our nature. We become arrogant and assertive, or submissive and dependent.

If the phenomenal wind is false, why do we not refuse to be affected by what we see and hear? *Māyā* is not false altogether. It is both true and untrue. Love is true and attachment is false. Truth is real and appearance is deceptive. Compassion is valuable, but it can make a person vain or it can be used as a cover to exploit another. Beauty is goodness, but sensual attraction can be a trap. Thus, all higher values have their counterfeits. We realize our mistake only after we experience the deception. It is hard to keep away from affectations.

Verse 77

paramoru viṇṇu paranna śakti kāṟṟā-
maṟivanalan jalamakṣamindriyārttham
dharaṇiyitiṅṅaneyañcu tattvamāy ni-
nneriyumitinte rahasyamēkamākum.

The one beyond is sky, the all-pervasive energy is wind,
knowledge is fire, senses are water, objects of interest
are earth; thus, as five principles,
this is ever blazing; the secret of this is one.

We have a beginning and an end. The beginning is not an event in time. It is a source like that of a fountain, causing our existence, growth and change as a resourceful basis. It is our ground, our substance. In the same manner, the end is also not an event that marks our extinction. It is the goal, the great magnet of life which is ever inspiring us to rise, to reach forward, to aspire, and it spells infinite possibilities.

In the present verse, the Guru presents the ground as the "One" which is the ground as well as the field, the scope as well as the function, and also the past, the present and the future. He refers to the sky as the ultimate, the beyond, the final cause which has the substance of transcendence. Like the inseparable beginning and end of a circle, the first and the final causes cancel out each other in the silence of the disappearance of enigmas and paradoxes when the meditator and the meditation blend and become one with the void of the unknown.

Between the first emergence of expereince to this world and the final exit from it there are a thousand and one chores to attend to, *koans* to solve, roles to play, tragedies and comedies to enact, conceptual worlds to create and boundaries to erect and smash. That is the world of energy, call it what you like: electromagnetism, thermodynamics, hydraulics, soul force, psychodynamics, libido or love-energy. From the small wisp of air that we breathe to the hurricane that can blow away a whole city, there are so many possibilities for air which actualizes as mind. If the verticality of perennial creation ranges between the ground and the sky beyond, it is horizontally filled with this energy to make the flux manifest.

The stuff of experience is like the warmth that keeps things going in hibernation, the gentle glow that reveals the contours of the mountain and the skyline at dusk or dawn, like the sparks that fly when the hammer beats against the anvil, the steady radiation of light from a spotlight, the leaping flames of fire that are eager to consume anything that comes their way, the all-embracing resplendence of the midday sun, and the fire that cooks, tempers, transforms and has the secret power of alchemy. The various shades of our knowledge can be compared to all these similes of fire. Therefore, Narayana Guru equates the fire with knowledge.

Like earth and water, our sensual interests and objects of interest intermingle. When we appreciate the glory of morning hues in the eastern sky the objectivity of the light cannot be disputed. A Vedic rishi, Blake, Pasternak or Tagore will forget everything before such a sight, while for many people there is "no time to stand and stare" at such glorious sights in this busy world of "getting and spending." Mere objectivity alone will not tickle the senses. There should be innate disposition which can seep into the object, as water penetrates a sod, to impregnate the object with the soul's delight or anguish. For this reason the Guru compares the senses to the element water and the objects of interest to earth.

After carefully assigning every limb of our experience its rightful place in the total sphere of the world of perennial becoming, the Guru asks us to share with him his unitive vision of the whole flux as a five-fold attribute of the One that is beyond all attributes.

Verse 78

maraṇavumilla puṟappumilla vāẓvum
nara surar ādiyumilla nāmarūpam
maruvil amarnna marīcinīru pōl ni-
lporu porul̤ām porul̤allitōrttiṭēṇam.

There is no death, or birth, or existence;
man, gods and all such are name and form;
what exists is like the water of a mirage in the desert–
it does not exist; this should be remembered.

Man seeks immortality. The fear of death is the greatest of all dreads. No one can overcome this fear by perpetuating the physical body as an imperishable substance. Deliverance from fear is always sought, and it is realized by arriving at truth and by recognizing it as the one value which makes the beautiful good and the good beautiful.

Death is a phenomenal experience of transformation. In one sense, it is a pause between two orders of functions in which a series of self-maintained and self-directed operations to preserve and continue the integrity of an organism is brought to a close and is then followed by a different mode of self-directed operations to disintegrate, disorganize and dissipate the organism into its more basic elements, from which the transformed substance can again enter into a fresh cycle of organized behaviour. A close look at death will reveal that it does not happen all at once. Within the body birth and death are happening simultaneously and continuously.

The births of new cells, new functions and new co-ordinations are all happening from moment to moment. If there is any truth in what modern physicists say about subatomic particles – bodies are emitted out of sheer nothingness and they are then devoured by antibodies – then, what we call birth, existence and death are only conventional suppositions. These suppositions are valid in a world of transactions. The horror of this validity can be somewhat mitigated for those fortunate ones who are able to turn their life-stream into a continuous symphony and a graceful dance attuned to an ingenious choreography designed by a master who has a perfect insight of the probability curve of the seeming chaos and randomness of the flux called world.

As it is impossible for most of us to dream of such a possibility, even in the wonderland of a utopia, we are left with only two alternatives. One is to turn away from this world and follow the footsteps of those masters and saviours who can show us the path to the Transcendent. In one sense or another, theistic Brahmanism, Judaism, Christianity, Islam and non-theistic disciplines like the Saṇkhyan's, the Taoist's and that of the Zen masters are all biased in favour of the transcendent. Philosophers like Kant have also given transcendence their best attention, and modern phenomenologists have improved upon it. The other alternative is to flow with the current of the flux without any special philosophy of life and be "*Les Miserables*". In this field one can also entertain himself with the jarring music of the existentialists by joining the choral song of anguish and nausea, and also realize how strong and irrefutable one's existence is when helplessness makes self-pity more than an obsession.

While Jean Paul Sartre thinks that man is cursed with his own freedom, even to the point of violating and hindering it, Narayana Guru avoids the dismal conclusions of the existentialist. Before leading us into the haven of deliverance, the Guru pauses for a moment in the favourite haunts of the phenomenologists to reconnoitre the crossroads on which, almost ritualistically, all philosophers stumble on an enigma and go round and round in the vicious circles perpetuated by tautology and contradiction. He does not tarry here long, however, because in the very next two verses he offers us his hand to surmount this hurdle, which St. John of the Cross compares to walking in the path of darkness, guided by darkness, to ultimately arrive before the darkest of all darkness, or to the ascending of Mount Carmel confronting nothing, nothing, nothing and expecting only nothing also on the summit.

Verse 79

janisamayam sthitiyilla janmiyanya-
kṣaṇamatil illitirippateprakāram?
hananavuminnane tanneyākayālē
jananavumillitu citprabhāvamellām.

At the time of birth there is no existence; the one who is born
is not in another moment; how can such a state be?
Death is also like this, and there is no birth;
everything is of the power of pure consciousness.

What is time? We see the sun appearing in the east, crossing the sky over our heads, and disappearing in the west. The locations of the sun on the eastern horizon and on the western horizon are imaginary. As many mathematical points can be marked on the surface of the earth, there can be as many points of location for a sunrise or a sunset. Nobody has ever bothered to watch the entire course of this movement. Occasionally people look up at the sky and notice a change in the position of the sun. We have, however, only an imaginary picture of this movement, which is not even one day long, but can be called to mind in a flash. Thus, an instantaneously presented image is our conceptual token of time. In this token, which we treat as real time, the seeming linear movement of the sun is deciphered and reconceived as a circular rotation of the earth on its imaginary axis without causing the slightest inconvenience to our mind for converting a perceptual imagery into a conceptual computerizing in order to arrive at a working postulate of time. Of course we do not think all these thoughts!

St. Augustine asks this question in *The Confessions:*

> I heard once from a learned man that the motions of the sun, moon and stars constituted time, and I assented not. For why should not the motions of all bodies rather be times? Or, if the lights of heaven should cease, and a potter's wheel run round, should there be no time by which we might measure those whirlings, and say, that either it moved with equal pauses...Or, while we were saying this,

should we not also be speaking in time?*

Why not? Is a potter's wheel too inefficient to mould time?

If time is the motion of things, what is the scale by which motion is measured? If we say that time is measured by motion and motion is measured by time, it is nothing short of begging the question. If a day is an abstraction of the picture of the sun's movement across the sky, what is night? How is it that we have juxtaposed day with night when our visual images of the two are contrary, and why do we bracket day and night into "one day"? If seeing the sun at different locations in the sky is essential to conceive the day, why is that requirement waived in order to conceive night?

Where should a man stand to notice the very first ray of the rising sun? If one man stands on the North Pole, one on the equator and another on the South Pole and all three stand on the same meridian, do they all see the sunrise simultaneously? If there is no simultaneity, which would be the ideal location on which to mark a standardized sunrise? It is well known that the earth's surface is irregular with mountains, valleys and oceans; if we are going to neglect these facts and just have a mathematical approximation of time, why should we want to give it a seeming objectivity?

What should we consider now: time, motion, an event, or a state of existence? If we agree to consider motion, then the motion of what? Is it the motion in space of the whole solar system along with the motions of other constellations and systems; or is it the motion of the earth around the sun, or the rotation of the earth on its imaginary axis; or is it the terrestrial or aerial movement of bodies from one location of space on earth to another; or is it the motion of the molecules with a static body, such as a rock in which the patterns of bumps, repulsions and attractions are so well-harmonized that for all practical purposes the stuff of the rock will remain uniform; or is it the motion of the electrons in their precisely ordained orbits around the nucleus; or is it the linear rush of a subatomic particle to bump on a similar subatomic particle so as to transform itself into a different category; or is it the wave of quantum mechanics? In other words, do we have any count of the systems we include, one within another ad infinitum, to conceive our notion of motion? The sensory perception of motion in the above-mentioned models is negligible. First of all, we conceive motion

* *The Confessions of St. Augustine,* Cardinal Edition, 1952, p. 230.

spatially and then, magically with a single stroke of imagination, we convert that into a non-spatial concept of relative duration. In this context, what is the physical or objective content of the word "time"?

Guru begins this verse with a reference to the time of birth. In this case birth can be seen as an event, an occurrence of something which was absent, or as the motion of a thing from an invisible area to a visible one, or it can be considered as a duration imagined by the mind in which a mathematical point is mentally marked to understand the continuity of motion in terms of discontinuous marks. All these three concepts are contrary to the notion of a static state of existence. What does exist for any duration of time if the galaxies, the solar system, the earth, bodies, molecules, and subatomic particles do not stay at any point of time and there is no discontinuity of motion at all?

In such a world of flux, we are trying to set up permanent, secure riches for ourselves at physical, biological, psychological and social levels. The result is constant upheavals. Origin, existence and death are equally imaginary. To avoid tragic frustrations and to have a well-balanced appreciation of the total perspective, the Guru, in this verse, gives us a secret key, which is to look at the whole picture as an adorable wonder, *cit prabhāvam ellām.*

A certain person sees This as a wonder,
likewise another speaks about This as a wonder.
Another hears of It even as a wonder,
but even hearing no one understands This at all.*

* *The Bhagavad Gita*, Chapter 2, Verse 29.

Verse 80

sthiti gati pōle virōdhiyāya sṛṣṭi-
sthiti layameṅṅoru dikkil ottu vāẓum?
gatiyiva mūnninumeṅṅumillitōrttāl
kṣiti mutalāyava gīru mātramākum.

Like rest and motion, how can contraries such as creation,
existence and dissolution coexist in one place?
There is no validity for these three anywhere; when this is
considered,
earth and such are mere words.

From the very first day of our recollection, we are aware of the constant sky which has always existed over our heads. Our good earth has not changed; we have the same sun, the same mountains and the same oceans. Each night the same constellations of stars reappear.

How can we say it is the same sky? When the earth is rotating on its axis and flying at great speed around the sun, how can we say that from our position on this space ship we are looking at the same sky? The sun and the other stars are supposed to be burning gases and leaping flames radiating energy. Is it the same light that falls into our eyes in two successive moments? Is there such a thing as a beam of light? Is it not just a collective expression referring to the bombardment of millions of photons? Has a photon any mass? No. Then how does it become a substance? According to physicists, it is just a plain electromagnetic wave, hv, of which h stands for Planck's constant and v for frequency. When such photons kick up the energy of 125,000,000 receptors, the impact is converged to 100,000 fibres of the *lovea centralis,* processed in an area of 15,000 square millimeters, and is then distributed into the relatively large area of the synapses of the visual brain. The resultant tumult, in which hundreds of thousands of molecules jump and dance around, is the awareness of seeing a ray of light. So when do we see the sun, or the stars or anything for that matter?

The *Īśāvāsya Upaniṣad* says:

Unmoving, the One is swifter than the mind.
The sense-powers reached not It, speeding on before,
Past others running, This goes standing.
In It Mātariśvan places action.

Robert Oppenheimer describes the probability pattern of the particle in the following words:

> If we ask for instance, whether the position of the electron remains the same, we must say 'No'; if we ask whether the electron's position changes with time, we must say 'No'; if we ask whether the electron is at rest, we must say 'No'; if we ask whether it is in motion, we must say 'No'.*

If this which describes the universe as a whole and a single particle in isolation is the truth, it can only be described as the indescribable. Hence, Guru says, "earth and such are mere words." The term used here for earth is *kṣiti.* Earth is also called *dhara. Dhara* means "that which gives everything its status to exist"; *kṣiti* means "that which destroys everything." Thus, this very earth is a meeting ground of creation and destruction. In the fictitious world of facts, or the factual world of fiction all shades of meaning burst into reality only as a conceptual awareness. If this is remembered, much of mind's unnecessary fuss and fume can be avoided.

* Robert Oppenheimer, *Science and the Common Understanding,* pp. 42-43.

Verse 81

prakṛti piriññorukūṟu bhōktṛ rūpam
sakalavumāy veḷiyē samullasikkum
ihaparamamoru kūṟidantayālē
vikasitamāmitu bhōgyaviśvamākum.

Prakṛti divides: on one side is the agent of enjoyment;
on the other, whatever shines outside
as the here and the beyond, as an expansion of thisness,
is the world of enjoyment.

When life becomes serious and I as a person face my real confrontation, I cease to be just one person among many. From me arises the overwhelming consciousness, "I am," and I stand in abeyance to respond or strike as the situation demands. For me, the situation becomes the "other," my only counterpart. The equation is "I am and this is."

In this context I am not a modest ego living in a finite body. I grow to an enormous size. My head rises above the clouds and my feet are planted in the very ground of the universe. It is as if I had roots reaching unfathomable depths. I extend in all directions and, lo, before me is the great wall of my confrontation. It can be he, she, it, or whatever. For me it is my "other" that springs into action as my inescapable challenge, my paramount confrontation. Here I am facing my destiny. It whispers, asks, shouts, scowls, screams, appeals, requests, whimpers, murmurs, stares, glances and goes into uncomfortable silence, leaving me to my own guesses. I distinctly hear every word articulated and not spoken: "I am your life. Do you accept me? Can you do justice to my trust, my expectation? Can you love me? Do you dare to reject me? Do you understand the secret of my spell, the worth of my values, my hidden mystery? What scares you? Do you have the courage to walk with me, to go the whole way with me?"

I become "I" only when I am confronted, doubted, trusted, questioned, loved, hated, endeared, estranged, accepted, rejected, insulted, or glorified. The "other" is the enjoyed, the only enjoyment that is. Everyone whom I have known thus far as "you," "she," "they" and everything known and unknown is now the "other." I am the one who sees it, hears it, smells it, touches it. Without me it has no existence that is either loved or hated, admired or condemned, accepted or rejected. "I" and the "other" are the two faces of the same coin. Here there is no God or man, no spirit or matter. There is only the nature of the enjoyer that enjoys, and the enjoyed in the arms of its enjoyer. From the infinitude of the cosmos to the finitude of the cup I hold to my lips, it is all one *bhogyavisvam*, the universe of enjoyment, and I am the sole enjoyer, the *bhoktṛ rūpam.*

Verse 82

araṇi kataññeẓumagni pōleyārā-
yvavaril irunnatiraṟṟeẓum vivēkam,
parama cidambaramārnna bhānuvāy ni-
nneriyumitinnirayāyiṭunnu sarvam.

Like fire that emerges from churning sticks,
the boundless discrimination that arises from contemplatives
burns as the sun that has attained the firmament of supreme consciousness;
to this everything is fuel.

Narayana Guru defines the Self as that which knows while remaining in the dark. When we are in deep sleep we do not know anything, but as soon as we wake up we experience consciousness pervading our body. Consciousness does not come from outside, it is always inside, even when we are asleep. As a person is aroused from deep sleep to wakeful consciousness, so can the wakeful mind be aroused to another degree of clarity. The Guru compares this to the churning of fire sticks to make a fire. Firewood is cold and inert, but when two sticks are rubbed against each other with force they emit fire, and this fire can ultimately burn away both sticks.

There are two factors in us which can be compared to two pieces of firewood in the churning process; they are the ego that enjoys and the world that is enjoyed. When a person enjoys something, he is unconsciously reducing his enjoying self and the object of his enjoyment to the homogenous principle of a conscious appreciation of value. In that value-appreciation both the "I" and the "other" vanish and their place is taken by a pure sense of happiness. In the previous verse, the Guru divided nature into two halves, the enjoyer and the enjoyed. In that division he conceived the enjoyer as inseparable from the enjoyed and as pervasive as the "other." In the present verse, he recommends that these two aspects should be critically scrutinized.

The ego is born of ignorance and so is the object of enjoyment. When an object is egoistically desired, this very desire obstructs the ego from seeing its own ground, which is nothing but pure happiness. The temporal, spatial and concrete specificity of the object provides a false ground for the projection of the Self's own happiness and perpetuates the consciousness of "otherness." The inquiry into the truth of both the self and the "other" is likened in this verse to the churning of fire sticks. When one submits oneself to the rigorous discipline of reflection, there emerges from such a person the bright light of discrimination which can dispel the ignorance that creates the false division of Self and non-Self. The emergence of wisdom in such unbounded measure has already been mentioned in earlier verses as the flaming sky of consciousness, or the rising of ten thousand suns in the sky of consciousness. In the present verse, Narayana Guru considers both the conditional self and its adjuncts of conditioning as the fuel for the great fire of unitive discrimination.

Verse 83

uṭayumirikkumudikkumonnu māṟi-
ttuṭarumitiṅṅuṭalin svabhāvamākum
muṭiyil irunnaṟiyunnu mūnnumātmā-
viṭaraṟumonnitu nirvikāramākum.

To break, to exist and to come into being is the nature of bodies here—
one goes, another takes its place;
remaining in the highest, the Self that knows all these three,
the indivisible one, is free of modifications.

We are now entering the last phase of our meditation on the Self. In this verse we are instructed to accept the reality of our physical limitations. Man's eternal prayer is to be led from non-existence to existence, from darkness to light and from death to immortality. Non-existence, darkness and death surround our physical existence in the body. Although the body looks whole and well-integrated, it is made up of billions of semi-autonomous units which are dying incessantly and are constantly replaced by similar units. As this process is going on in an unconscious state, we do not know anything about either the growth or the deterioration of the body. Eventually when the dead and decomposed cells or similar units are no longer being replenished, we begin to recognize the ageing process. Finally it comes to a breaking point and the whole physical system collapses.

The physical body is a biochemical modulation in the on-flowing stream of life on earth. It is entirely subject to natural laws. Nature makes short-term provisions for the continuation of life in the body and long-term provisions for the continuation of a species through the serialization of proliferated life units. In both the short-term and the long-term prolongations of life, the systems adopted by nature have the triple principle of origination, sustentation and dissolution. In the long-term series, the living essence of one body is transmitted to another in the form of progeny. Children continue the life of their parents. If in some sense the theory of evolution has validity, we have to admit that all forms of life are modifications of the one biologic principle. The continuity of life on earth can be understood only in terms of incessant birth, existence and dissolution, and the same organic stuff is then consumed in the generation of another life. Our physical growth and sustenance are derived from the nourishment we get from food, and the food on our table was a living organism a couple of hours, days or weeks before it was processed into food. In one form or another we will also change into food for other beings, or into manure for the vegetative world. If this is all that happens, life has only little meaning and we don't need to uphold our morale or to dedicate our life to any high purpose.

Not everything in our life happens in the dark recesses of the unconscious. All through life we experience and enjoy the self-luminous glow of our consciousness. Like the fire that remains latent in firewood, and the detailed plan of a tree that hides as a potential in its seed, the Self is enveloped by the veil of the non-Self. It does not originate or dissolve. Nature, which is subject to transformation, derives its intelligence and its laws from the imperishable light of the Self. True immortality is not achieved by perpetuating the physical body or by producing a progeny, it is attained by knowing the Self. The potter, who handles a lump of clay to make a pot, is conscious of the breaking and kneading of the sod, of its transformation into a pot, of the aesthetic value of the pot he makes, and he recognizes the same clay even when the pot breaks into pieces. The apparent transformations of the clay that the potter observes are called *vikāra.* Although the clay is transformed and has a new name and form when it is temporarily recognized as a pot, the new name and form do not affect the substantial nature of the clay. So we can say that the clay continues to be in a *nirvikāra* state, or a state of non-becoming.

In the present verse, the Self is qualified as *nirvikāra* and it is further described as *viṭararum,* which means "without any cleavage." The consciousness that animates a living body is very elusive and hard to understand. Physical ailments such as brain diseases and nervous debilities can cause serious aberrations in the normal and healthy functioning of consciousness. Physiologically it can easily be shown that consciousness cannot prevail without a biochemical and biophysical basis. For that reason, immortality cannot be achieved by any fancied perpetuation of consciousness. Consciousness of the mind is as ephemeral as the body. There is an astounding ontologic reality of consciousness, however, which can be seen implied in the origin and function of all bodies, ranging from a subatomic particle to a galactical system. The mind of man must be a participant in the cosmic intelligence which rules the entire universe if it is capable of calculating, of deriving equations, of mathematically conceiving the distance between the earth and other planets, of jettisoning a spaceship across hurdles, like the breaking away form earth's orbit and the entering into the orbit of another planet to finally land on it, and capable of making contrivances for the spaceship to flash back to earth its physical data as accurately as it can be done in a laboratory on earth.

It is this intelligent Self that is the imperishable reality. We are that, so there are no fresh problems of immortalization. As we recognize our oneness with this rich ontologic verity of the intelligent being in us, it becomes easy for us to remain in that peak position as impassive witnesses of all that goes on at the physical level of nature and not get carried away by the sentiments roused by the triple states of birth, existence and death. Realization is a matter of knowing and not of becoming.

Verse 84

arivatināl avanī vikāramuṇṭe-
nnaruḷumitōrkkil asatyamuḷḷaturvī;
niravadhiyāy nilayarru nilpatellā-
marivil eẓum prakṛti svarūpamākum.

As modifications of earth are known, it is said that they exist–
this is untrue when considered; what exists is earth;
the countless entities remaining without foundation
are all innate forms of nature existing in knowledge.

We see clay and we recognize it to be clay. In the same manner, we see a pot and recognize that to be a pot. So what is there that is unreal in a pot? There is a subtle distinction between the two cases of perception mentioned above. The principle of discrimination that is to be employed in either case is overlooked if we say that both perceptions are of the same order. If a potter wants to know how much clay he has used in one day, he is not interested in the many articles he has created, in fact, he will treat all his pots and pans as clay and he will enter in his cash book the purchase of a cartload of clay. The same potter, however, will not give much thought to the homogeneity of the clay which he moulded into jars, pots and pans, when he is at his sales counter; there he will ask his customers to pay special attention to the tasteful display of form which distinguishes one pot from another. Thus, each occasion warrants a special emphasis on the principles of discrimination.

The pot, as was already mentioned in the previous verse, is a *vikāra*, or a modulation given to the shape of the clay. The ultimate reality out of which this world is modulated is pure knowledge. The dynamics of modulation is called *prakṛti* (nature). *Prakṛti* is constituted of three *guṇas,* which are the attributes of knowledge (*sattva*), motion (*rajas*) and rest or inertia (*tamas*). The *guṇas* are capable of fixing the individual mind's attention at any degree between absolute reality and total falsehood. If a person does not know how to discriminate between the real and the unreal, it is very likely that he will fall into snares of confusion even at the empirical level. Delighted by the splendour of light, moths fly into the blazing fire. When an elephant rubs its forehead on a rugged rock it gets a pleasant feeling of itchiness and, believing that this delight comes from the rock, it goes on rubbing until its skin is torn and its head bleeds. The fish that mistakes bait for food is caught by the angler, and snakes, enchanted by the musician's pipe, dance their way into captivity. Man is also subject to the same kind of deluding infatuation.

The modulations that come from nature can direct an individual mind in the two opposite directions of truth and untruth. We cannot say whether our daily life is objective or subjective. We may call the same earth *dharitri*, terra firma, or *avanī*, the abode, or any other epithet that may reflect the special meaning we have in mind to suit a particular occasion. These are all conceptual or nominal images which we project on earth pure and simple. The gestalt psychologist says that we see only what we want to see; there is great truth in that.

Of the three dynamics of nature none is inferior to the other. *Sattva* presents in a clear transparent way the exact nature of a thing in terms of knowledge; the inertia and opacities of *tamas* can stabilize and fix an entity into a concrete existence; and *rajas* is capable of mixing consciousness (*cit*) and inertia (*jada*) into different shades of translucency with varying degrees of objectivity and subjectivity. The chair and the table we use are there as solid pieces, and in that case inertia is of immense value. A physicist can prove that a solid table is only an appearance of what is in fact a mass of flying molecules and, within his own frame of reference, he is right. This, however, does not make the table any less solid or undependable for pragmatic utility. If we see cakes and ice cream served on a similar table on a television screen, we can only admire the sight but cannot taste the cakes. We can of course appreciate the picture on the screen more than a blank wall in a dark room. Thus, whatever modulation comes it has relative merit and demerit.

To exercise proper discrimination, one should have the normative notion of the Self as one's guiding principle. The Self is pure knowledge, and boundless are the modulations which arise from the triple function of the attributes of nature – knowledge, flux – like motion and inertia. These functions are to be treated as the negative attributes of the otherwise attributeless Absolute.

Verse 85

niẓal oru bimbamapēkṣiyāte nilpī-
leẓumulakeṅṅumabimbamākayālē
niẓalumatallitu nērumalla vidvā-
neẓutiyiṭum phaṇi pōle kāṇumellām.

No shadow exists independent of an actual form;
as there is no original form anywhere for the existing world,
it is neither shadow nor substance;
everything that is seen is like a snake painted by a master.

Of all philosophic problems, none has caused more dispute among thinkers than the judging of the right distinction between appearance and reality. Philosophers have made this problem even more complex by drawing a line between what "seems to be" and what "looks."

> There are at least two groups of appearance idioms – what might be called "seeming idioms" and "looking idioms." The first group typically includes such expressions as "appears to be," "seems to be," "given the appearance of being"; the second, such expressions as "appears," "looks," "feels," "tastes," "sounds."*

In Plato's *Republic,* Socrates makes a division in knowledge between what appears to be falling on the "eyeball" or the "sky ball." According to him, all we see here are only shadows of archetypal ideas. In this verse, Narayana Guru refuses to accept the Platonic theory of shadows. For a shadow to appear there needs to be a concrete object or body to obstruct or reflect the light. If the world of our experience is the shadow of another world, that world should have an existence elsewhere. We do not know of any existence other than what is experienced here and now.

There are many variations of shadow. When a concrete body stands in the path of light, a dark patch is cast on the ground or on a wall and

* *The Encyclopedia of Philosophy,* Vol. I, p. 135.

that is called a shadow. We can easily distinguish the shadow of a man from that of a tree or a dog and the careful manipulation of shadows that can make them closely resemble actual people. The reflections we see on oil or water are more detailed than mere dark shadows, however, they too are only shadows. In a well-polished mirror we see the clearest of all images, except that the right looks like the left and the left looks like he right. In the projection of cinerama, one can experience the illusion of walking into the panorama and among the people that are projected, but realistic as this might seem, we cannot have any transactions with these projected shadows.

In comparison to all these shadows, the encounter of actual persons and objects is a most real experience, and this is where we come to the real stumbling block. We have no means of apprehending the physical world except through our sense impressions. Although we are experiencing the seemingly infinite magnitude of the universe, all forms of perception are manufactured for us within our own small skulls. Neurophysiologists, who have busied themselves with the inner mechanism of perception, are yet to discover how exactly the electrical impulses that agitate the synapses of the brain can reproduce a world of colour, sound, name and form, and magnify it according to a standardized perspective which seems to be of a measure identical to the images produced by the brain-stuff in all skulls, whether of a man, a rabbit or a frog. If the cosmos we experience is the image of an image of an image, what means do we have to verify it as bona fide?

Narayana Guru's answer to this question is that in this context such a criterion is not feasible. All that he agrees to is that a continuous process of gestaltation is going on and that the expertise involved in it is matchlessly superb. He compares the world the world to a snake painted by a master. If the painting is realistic enough, the image of the snake can cause fright, but as it is only a picture, after the first shock one will realize that it is only an appearance. That knowledge brings an altogether different appreciation of the same picture. Now the picture is admired for its beauty, and one might even want to possess it as a remarkable aesthetic expression. In either case, we are affected by the compelling aesthetics of the picture. This world also offers us a similar ambivalence of repulsion and attraction. On the whole, it is a source of continuous affection.

Verse 86

tanu mutalāyatu sarvamonnil onni-
llanṛtavumāy atināleyanyabhāgam
anudinamastamiyātirikkayālē
punar ṛtarūpavumāy poliññiṭunnu.

The body and all similar things have no being one in another,
and become untrue for that reason; another part,
remaining without setting from day to day,
once again, as the true form, attains perfection.

Things appear as separate entities, such as a man or a dog, a pen or a book, a cup or a saucer. The body of a thing has its own special qualities which makes it unique and different from other bodies. When a body perishes, its existence terminates and it does not continue in the existence of another body. For example, grandfather is different from father and father is different from son, and when one of them dies his existence is not transferred to his progeny. Their essential difference and individuality belong to their bodily existence, and however real they might look or however dynamically they might assert themselves all will die, one by one in the course of time. Thus, their physical existence proves to be a transient phenomenon.

Even when a chair or a cup breaks, the idea of the chair or the cup does not break, and the names "chair" and "cup" will continue, unaffected by the physical destruction of those items. Similarly, when a person such as the Buddha ceases to exist physically, he does not vanish altogether from our memory. In fact, in his case, his individual existence has changed into a universal existence. Two complementary principles in physics are the conservation of matter and the transformation of energy. The matter that has gone into the making of a man or a chair or a cup cannot turn into nothingness, it simply undergoes a transformation and continues as indestructible matter. Thus, materially, conceptually and nominally, everyting continues even after the empirical distintegration of the perceptual body-content.

All cups come under the same category—cups. Thus, the exclusiveness of a thing ceases and it becomes participatory in a class that continues to function. A truth that can function with an operational dynamic is called *ṛtam*. Thus, all bodies have two aspects: the perishable, when each object is taken by itself, and the imperishable, when it is taken materially, conceptually or nominally. The perishable aspect is called *anṛtam* and the perishable aspect is called *ṛtam*.

Our vexations are caused by the *anṛtam* to which we are exposed. When we rely on something to function forever in an individual capacity, we receive an abrupt shock at the sudden seizure of that individual entity. This entity could be one's father or mother, husband or wife, automobile or refrigerator, one's typist or typewriter. The physical death of one's parents or spouse can be overlooked if one accepts the reality of their continuous presence in one's loving heart. The automobile can be towed to a service station for repairs or it can be replaced, and one can hire a new typist and get a new typewriter. This does not mean that there is no room for the delicate sentiments one might feel for one's typist or automobile, they are the poetic embellishments of one's psyche.

A person living a life without exaggerations can always overcome the disasters caused by the perishing aspect of bodies, and he can continue to be in harmony with the rhythm of the world order by faithfully holding on to the imperishable, the unified whole.

Verse 87

taniyeyitokkeyumuṇṭu tammil ōrō-
rinamitaraṅṅaḷil illayiprakāram
tanu mutalāyatu sattumallayōrttā-
lanṛtavumallatavācyamāyiṭunnu.

Taking each kind alone, it exists;
mutually, each excludes the other;
when this is remembered, body and all such
are neither real nor unreal; that is indescribable.

Our experience can generally be divided into two aspects – looking and seeing. The looking aspect is usually recognized as the subject and the seeing aspect as the object. One might be led to think that the subject is inside and the object is outside. This, however, is not so. Spinoza speaks of the nature that natures. Similarly, knowledge has a rigorous incentive to know, and its fields of interest are many, such as the physical, the chemical, the biologic, the social, the historic, the linguistic, the artistic, the musical and so on. When consciousness is directed to any particular field it confines itself to the one class it selected, choosing one species in that class, and within that species it might concentrate on a sub-species and then on the characteristic marks or qualities of its individual entities. Mind functions both analytically and synthetically. Consciousness vacillates between what is seen and the motivational urge. At the analytical level the mind is with a thing or an individual.

As an individual, Peter is different from Paul. Each individual has his or her own separate life and personal qualities, thus, in that sense, one person can never become an exact substitute for another. As an individual entity undergoes transformations during the course of time, its functional reality, or *ṛtam*, cannot be considered uniform and universal. Lack of conformity and universality puts the entity under the category of the transient. The duration of existence can be one millionth of a second or a hundred millennia, but that does not change the status of a thing which has only a finite existence. Whatever is finite in its duration is unreal.

Individuality is not the only reality. Peter, Paul and John can all be included in the class called "man," and Mary, Ruth and Sarah come in the class called "woman." They can all be included in a general class called "humanity," and although lions and monkeys cannot be included in this group, man can join them in a class called "animal." Animals, birds and vegetation can all go under the even more general classification of "living beings."

The entire world stands divided between genus and species. In the present verse the word *inam* is translated as "kind," but in another work entitled *Jatilakṣana,* Narayana Guru elaborates the meaning of *inam* by saying that what distinguishes the individuality of one from another is called "kind." If there were no kinds, we could not conceive things, it would in fact be as though there was nothing. Formal individuations rise from the depth of consciousness one after another, like waves appearing on the surface of the ocean. It is in the mould of knowledge that the cast of every individuation is produced.

As an example of "kind," the Guru points out the characteristics one may notice in the biologic world in which each species has its own kind of body, appearance, sound, smell, temperature and taste. Except in the case of lower forms of life, each kind has its own males and females for mating and reproducing. Those who cannot mutually mate and reproduce are not of the same kind. Thus, in the world of transactions, the embodiment of a being or a thing is very important. However, when we closely scrutinize a thing or a being that has a gross body it proves to be only in a transitory phase. For instance, when a candle burns its entire body disappears leaving no traces anywhere; thus, its grossness and its form are easily convertible into invisible gaseous entities. Some potted plants require no manure; they grow fabulously with just a little moisture, some light and materials they gather from the air; it is as if they can produce all the matter required for their foliage and stems out of nothing. Thus, what is visibly present as a concrete entity disappears, and, in the same manner, invisible forms of energy manifest into concrete entities. These transient formal factors are not true in the sense that they have a beingness which corresponds to their visual form, as all kinds are entirely dependent on their form and placement. In what Husserl calls regional ontology, they are only appearances.

For the above reason, in this verse Narayana Guru treats kinds as unreal, but at the same time, in the factual world of life situations, every kind that constitutes a system has a structural relevancy and a functional reality and therefore we cannot say that the kinds are altogether unreal. In this context the Guru recognizes the functional validity of things, and, as it is contradictory to say that the kinds are substantially unreal and functionally real, to avoid such conflict he calls them indescribable.

Verse 88

sakalavumuḷḷatu tanne tattvacintā-
grahan itu sarvavumēkamāy grahikkum;
akamukhamāy aṟiyāykil māyayām van-
paka palatum bhramamēkiṭunnu pāram.

Everything is real in itself; one who grasps the basic truth
will understand all this as one;
if not known introspectively,
māyā's great enmity certainly creates much confusion.

In the preceding eighty-seven verses many aspects of the Self and the world have been dealt with. After considering all these expositions, if one has a calling to fulfil his obligations in the workaday world, insisting on the reality of transactions, no one can tell him that the world does not exist. In this verse Narayana Guru agrees with such a person by saying that in a transactional sense everything has existence. In the transactional world the polarization is between "I" and "this"; the cognizing consciousness of the individual is on one side and on the other are the countless entities that can be treated as the "other." As it has been pointed out already, there are two kinds of visions, *anya* and *sama*. Seeing each thing separately is called *anya*, which fixes the status of a separate object, and seeing everything as one is called *sama*.

A person who sees everything as one is referred to in this verse as a *tattvacintāgrahan*, meaning the philosopher. This Sanskrit term is very suggestive, it can be split into *tat + tvam + cinta + grahan*. *Tat* means "that all-inclusive reality which transcends the scope of being treated discursively"; *tvam* means "you and whatever is experienced by you," or, in other words, the content of your consciousness which is the world that you transact with or relate to; *cinta*, in the present context, means "contemplative reasoning"; and *grahan* means "a person who grasps the conclusions of his ponderings." Such being the qualifications of a philosopher, it is no wonder that he sees everything in this world as belonging to the one reality.

In the Upanisads there are four well-known dictums which are called *mahāvākyas.* One of these is *tat tvam asi,* "that thou art." This is also called the dictum of instruction. As a novice in philosophy is expected to meditate on this dictum, he can justifiably be called *tattvacintāgrahan,* one who has properly discerned the relationship between the Absolute and the relative world.

Objects in the external world are varied and separate, or at least that is how we treat them. "What is wrong with that natural disposition?" One might ask. The answer is somewhat complex. Unity is the essential nature of everything and somehow everything is held together by a force of attraction. This is true of the galactical system and of the molecular universe. What is true of matter in this respect is also true of consciousness. One person is attracted to another because of their essential unity, but, as they outwardly seem to have separate bodies, the idea of the "other" comes to both of them and they desire the other, or at least one desires the other. Desire is a great source of trouble. A person is not tormented by a desire for his own legs or his hands, as they are already his and he treats them all as organically one. Similarly, a person does not desire his parents to be his because that factor is to him an undisputed reality. One can, however, feel great attachment for one's parents and great pain may be experienced on the eve of a separation from them, caused by death or otherwise. This attachment is born of the idea of the "other," and besides desire and attachment, the idea of the "other" can also cause hatred, greed, lust, anger and fear. In this verse, Narayana Guru calls these the revengeful acts of *māyā.*

Māyā is another name for *prakṛti. Prakṛti* is constituted of *satva, rajas* and *tamas.* The nature of *satva* is to spotlight a value; *rajas* makes the mind fascinated with the value highlighted by *satva* and it infatuates the mind with the relativistic colouration; and *tamas* binds the mind to the object of infatuation and causes an inertial opacity which blunts the vision of value, and, as the light goes, the desired object becomes a meaningless burden. Nature repeats this series by turning the mind to yet another object of desire. A wisdom seeker desires to free himself from the fetters of nature.

Nature's laws cannot be violated. Seeking the Absolute while living in the relativistic situations of nature is as hard a task as the navigating of a boat upstream against the current of the river. To attempt such a hazardous enterprise, one should know all the intricacies of nature, as nature favours one who knows all her secrets, but does not pardon any mistakes whatsoever. The gravitational pull to earth is a law of nature and hydraulic pressure is another law of nature. If, by firing jet fuel, one can put enough pressure on a heavy body to surpass the gravitational pull, that heavy body can rise into the sky. Thus, by using two laws of nature we can control the flight of aircrafts; however, the slightest mistake can make the plane crash or blow up. This kind of insight is applicable to all the transactions in which nature is involved.

Narayana Guru does not stop a person from his mundane pursuits or from carrying out his transactions, but, in his infinite compassion, he cautions people to be aware of the harsh laws of nature so that they can be used for their own advantage, mundane as well as spiritual.

Verse 89

arivil irunnasadastiyennasaṅkhyam
poriyiḷakibbhuvanam sphurikkayālē
arivine viṭṭoru vastuvanyamille-
nnariyaṇamīyarivaika rūpyamēkum.

Existing in knowledge, as the being of non-being,
countless sparks arise, causing the appearance of the world;
so, apart from knowledge there is not another thing;
thus one should know; this knowledge bestows the state of
oneness.

To examine truth and to arrive at certitudes scientists depend mainly on experimental verifications. In an experiment, a hypothesis is postulated and the scientist observes it under varying conditions, but until it is proved fruitful the postulate is *a priori*. In Vedanta philosophy, as in other fields of spiritual discipline, analogy plays the same role of experimental verification. In essence, both experiments and analogies are examples. In the present verse, Narayana Guru gives us a comprehensive example which contains various valuable suggestions. These suggestions are called *lakṣaṇas* (marks) and each of these marks has its scope which is called *vyāpti*.

Narayana Guru analogically compares this world to an ensemble of sparks flying from the fire of consciousness or knowledge. Each spark has an origin, a period of existence and an extinction. It moves continuously from the moment of its origin to that of its extinction and finally it turns to ashes. We are like these sparks.

The one fire is the common source of all sparks. It is hard to ascertain how and when the thermal principle of fire began and it is difficult to decide the magnitude of its field. Fire has many aspects, and in this verse it is equated with consciousness, the consciousness that is asserting the individuality of the sparks by illuminating each bit of carbon. As a potential it is not visible, yet, without producing flames, it can manifest to a large extent as the temperature of the atmosphere and of the living bodies of animals. It becomes visible only when it leaps into flames. Thus, consciousness also has a very wide and deep base buried in the unconscious. Every aspect of knowledge is a specific manifestation, like the flames of fire. The sparks symbolize the transient and the individuated aspect of every autonomous unit in the world of physical manifestation.

On reading these pages one's eyes run over the written letters. A letter does not seem to be anything other than carbon dust sticking to white paper, yet something besides the impression of the ink can be seen. Each letter suggests the articulation of a certain sound, and groups of letters flash to the mind a word that has meaning. These letters are like glowing sparks. The ink as such connotes nothing, it is the form of the letter that suggests a meaning, and what is true of this letter is also true of everything we perceive. From a period or a comma marked on this page to the whole universe, nothing is but a form suggesting a meaning. A form, however, cannot stand by itself, it should have a medium. This can be something concrete like the earth, or flowing like water, luminous like fire, gaseous as air, or it can give location like space, sequence like time and ideation like consciousness.

Sparks are either burning pieces of carbon or molecules of matter. These tiny pieces, whether carbon of matter, do not have the quality of luminosity; it is the burning fire that glows and we cannot separate the glow from the burning matter. When we read a written word the glow of meaning belongs to the ink-stain, they cannot be separated.

The real and the unreal thus belong together in making each unit of awareness. Each item of experience is an awareness of something. There is no way of postulating the existence of anything anywhere without making it an object of awareness. Although each spark has an individuality of its own, the glowing fire in each belongs to one and the same luminous principle. In the same way, everything that we experience would be unitively understood as belonging to the one consciousness, which is none other than the Self.

The ontologic richness of fire is meagre in a spark, as, even though it is fire in principle, it does not promise a wholesale participation with the universal fire of which it is a part. In the same manner, the mere glow of consciousness experienced by our mind cannot secure an identification with the universal Self for us unless we know how to link the individual manifestation with its universal basis.

To effect such union Śankara suggests a continuous meditation of the true nature of the Self, which he terms *svasvarūpa anusandhāna.* He takes it for granted that one's true nature is that of the Self, which is pure existence (*sat*), knowledge (*cit*) and peerless bliss (*ānanda*). Ramanuja does not like to leave the quality of bliss vague and recommends meditating on the blissful state of the Self which he calls *svarūpānanda*. Madhva takes it further, he makes constant comparison between the personal experience of happiness and the unbounded happiness of the Supreme Lord; this he terms *svarūpānanda tāratamya*.

Although the three masters seem to be of different opinions, Narayana Guru effects an integration of their views in his analogy of the manifested world as an ensemble of sparks. In verse 33 the Guru made reference to knowledge changing and becoming all these things; he compared it to fire circles caused by the brandishing of a burning torch in several figure of 8 movements. In another work called *Aṟivu*, "The epistemology of gnosis" (verses 12-15), the Guru describes how knowledge sparks off.

Yourself is what is known as knowledge;
By putting down your own knowledge, it becomes the known.
The known is thus twofold: one conscious of knowing
And the other not conscious of the same.

Knowledge, too, likewise in its turn proceeding
Became reflected in the knower once again
And one spark of knowledge falling into this the known
Into five shreds it became split up.

If one could still be cognizant of oneself
As the knower of knowledge, still knowing knowledge to be all,
The one that is knowledge and the one that is the knower
Within that which is known, six and eight, too, they become.

Corresponding likewise with this known
Knowledge, too, seven and one, makes eight;
knowledge is thus superficially distinguished
As also the known, when separated one from one.

First the Guru divides consciousness into two, the knower and the known. He then splits the known into five sensory awarenesses and he subdivides the knower into mind, intellect and ego. In fact, each of these, when considered as a spark, can be further visualized as separate universes constituted of countless millions of sparks accounting for experiences of all sorts. The link between sparks of consciousness and their source, the Self, is the golden thread of a sense of endearment which connects all values that are recognized as a repeated illumination of the natural bliss of the Absolute mirrored by each spark-like occasion.

Verse 90

anṛtamorastitayē maṟaykkukille-
nnanubhavamuṇṭu sadastiyennivannam
anupadamastitayāl itāvṛtam sad-
ghanamatināle kaḷēbarādi kāryyam.

The unreal does not conceal what exists,
such is the experience; what exists is; in this way,
at every step this is enveloped by existence;
therefore, body and such effects are existence through and through.

Everything that constitutes our experience has an ontologic reality. This reality consists of an innate structure that has its correspondence to a coordinated function. The structure and the function, when taken together, give the existing thing an undeniable reality. This is, so to say, the anatomic frame of the entire universe which enables it to function harmoniously. It is called *ṛtam* and it is not confined to any one thing, in fact, the inner structure and function of a thing is complementary to many other things. The beauty, the fragrance, the structure of the petals, the placement of honey in the calyx and the special design of a flower are the exact requirements to attract the bee or a butterfly to fertilize it, while the insect relishes the honey. Thus, there is a complementarity between two entirely different species for the continuance of both.

This kind of interrelationship between all living forms reveals *ṛtam.* The universal order of functional harmony can be easily observed, such as day and night, the varying temperature of the sun, the clouds that bring rain and the gaseous constitution of the atmosphere, all of which help perpetuate life on earth. Everything, from subatomic particles to the mightiest stars, is linked to this ontologic law of mutual subsistence, and the microscopic verity of the *ṛtam* is as real as its macrocosmic validity. This innate law, however, can at times be misunderstood and cause great confusion, as for instance when one mistakes a rope for a snake, or mother-of-pearl for silver. This kind of mistake is called *anṛtam.* In our interpersonal relationship we might project on another qualities that he or she does not possess and later come to grievous frustration. Such confusion, caused by *anṛtam,* does not remain undetected for long; sooner or later one finds out one's mistake. Some can deceive some people some time, but all people cannot deceive all people all the time. If a man pretends to be an enginner, a physician, or a chartered accountant, he might get away with it till he is put into a crucial situation where he has to show his efficiency in the particular trade he professes, but his inefficiency will reveal him to be a hoax. In the *Bhavad Gita* it is said that one should never attempt to do anything for which he has no natural aptitude. Pretension brings fear.

In all situations of cognition, action and appreciation, the ontologic reality of the situation comes both from the I-consciousness and its objective counterpart. The viability of cognition, action and appreciation confirms the reality of whatever constitutes the experiential situation; it is as if truth envelops everything and confirms it to be so again and again. As the source of reality is the same in all experiences, we can say that all positive experience is of the same existential truth which is identical with the Self.

In the *Apavāda Darśana* of the *Darśana Māla,* Narayana Guru says that if this world is affirmed to be real, then it is existential, and if the reality of the phenomenal world is denied, its truth becomes subsistential. As both the knower and the known have existential validity, it can be concluded that what is seen as the psychophysical reality in the here and now of life are all effects of the one supreme existence.

Verse 91

priya viṣayam prati ceytiṭum prayatnam
niyatavumaṅṅane tanne nilkkayālē
priyamajamavyayamaprameyamēkā-
dvayamitutan sukhamārnnu ninniṭunnu.

Whatever effort is made in relation to each
object of endearment it remains ordained;
this dear value – unborn, unspent, unpredictable, one without a second –
remains established in happiness.

Life is a continuous series of releasing and directing forces to obtain, precipitate or perpetuate happiness. An object, a person, a situation, or an event becomes an object of interest when one visualizes in any of them a potential form of happiness. The interest automatically releases a chain of action to actualize the potential.

In the world of mechanics the operation of a force can be one of conservation, as when a body is static, or it can be one of motion when action is required. The action of a living being is akin to the spreading of the total momentum of its psychophysical energy into areas that are physically or psychically relevant to place the individual in a comfortable position from which to derive the maximum happiness a situation can yield. Barring miscalculations that can misfire and cause undesired reactions, all the ontologically valid matchings of one's desire with the desired always assure the actualization of one's happiness.

Although each individual item of interest and its actualization are shortlived, the principle of the quest for happiness, the direction of energy to actualize it and the process by which the potential becomes actual belong to an innate law of the world order. The existence and the operation of this law – that all objects of interest always evoke effort on the part of whoever desires anything – is exemplified by the incessant searching of all individuals, which results in either realization or frustration. Not having an overt or positive desire is also a desire to be, or to withhold, or to withdraw. We think we are absolutely actionless when we are in deep sleep, but watching a person in deep sleep will soon explode this myth.

In verse 90 the ontologic verity of absolute existence was highlighted, and our transactional world was put on the stable foundation of valid comprehension of the real, within the frame of reference of a relativistic world of individual entities. In that verse the emphasis was on the existential validity of things, whether they were of a physical, psychological or cosmological order. In this verse the focus is on values that, by complementing the passing moments of living beings, can bring to the individual a mode of happiness that can to some degree approximate one's perfection. In other words, the topical interest of the present verse is the teleological pursuit in which, consciously or unconsciously, all living beings are engaged.

Although the value that catches one's fancy for practical attention is apparently of a transient order, as a value it participates in the basic blissful essence of the Self. The Self is not transient and hence its essence is beginningless and endless, indivisible and one without a second; it eludes the comprehension of all relativistic minds. Even though this highest of values is of an elusive nature, all relative objects of interest become enduring to the individual because of the all-pervading nature of the Self, without which nothing can exist, nothing can be known and nothing can be experienced as either painful or pleasure-giving.

The Self alone is. It is existent, subsistent and bliss.

Verse 92

vyayamaṇayāte veḷikku vēlaceyyum-
niyamamirippatukoṇṭu nityamākum
priyamakamē piriyāteyuṇṭitinnī
kriyayoru kēvalabāhyaliṅgamākum.

Unexpended, the law of action operates outside;
therefore, it is eternal;
within, endearment is inseparable;
to this, action is only an external symbol.

Water never tires of making ripples, and fire leaps into flames at the slightest chance to create a conflagration. Atoms like to twirl, and it is the sport of earth to rotate on its axis and revolve around the sun. The universe is as busy as a beehive, everything moves and changes and becomes something else. All these motions and happenings can go under one blanket phrase, "the phenomenon of change and becoming." Each individual movement seems to be locally generated and a trifle, compared to the ceaseless evolutions of the cosmos. In this verse the principle of becoming is treated as a grand generalization of all the factual operations that are going on.

The capacity to function is what makes a thing exist in a certain category. When it stops functioning in one capacity, then we can be sure that it has already changed into another category, and it is functioning in another way without leaving the mainstream of phenomenal change. Thus, on the whole, becoming is coeternal with being.

Man is an integral part of the world of becoming. His contributions to change are chronicled by historians, excavated by archeologists, and can be directly seen in the sprawling cities around us and their networks of roads, in the changing panorama of the landscape, and in the hustle-bustle of the transportation system in the sky, the earth and the ocean. Man's fancy even goes to the extent of putting satellites in the orbits of planets, and of sending wandering robots to reconnoitre the milky way.

We do not know why water flows, or why fire burns, why the wind blows, or the sun shines, but we do know why man works day in and day out busying himself over so many endeavours. It pleases him. He is motivated. Like the phenomenal change that never abates for a moment, the desire of man to be repeatedly pleased in new ways also continues as the one quest that keeps him on the track of action from birth to death. When one man leaves his work, another man picks it up. The tradition of a generation has its continuators in the next.

Thus, we have two parallel streams of change flowing from eternity to eternity. One is the purpose of action, the meaning of change, the cause that transmutes into effect, the motivational force that causes restlessness to a soul, the desire to be happy, the response to challenges, the urge to bring order to chaos, the desire to effect harmony and the will to create; this is the inner stream which every man recognizes as the one desire of his heart. The other is the external stream, the phenomenon of change, the man in action, the world that devours the dead to spew newborn beings. The outer phenomenon of action is a visual symbol which reveals the meaning of the quest that is hidden until it is actualized.

Verse 93

calamuṭal aṟṟa tanikku tanteyātmā-
vilumadhikam priya vastuvillayanyam;
vilasiṭumātmagatapriyam viṭāṭī
nilayil irippatukoṇṭu nityamātmā.

To one detached from the changing body,
nothing is more dear than his self;
as the self-oriented value continuously remains
in this state, the Self is eternal.

In one sense, we are living two realities at the same time. Our physical reality is one of constant change in which there is no reversal of anything that perishes. The process of ageing is the same. Childhood, adolescence, youth, middle age, old age and death follow one after another and there is no reversibility in this series, but the I-identity, which becomes formulated almost at the wake of our consciousness, remains unaffected throughout our life. Although we have no consciousness of a personal identity in deep sleep, when we wake, the lapse of I-consciousness during that state does not cause any sense of discontinuity either in our beingness or in our personality. Psychic and assumed contrasting moods, such as hilarity or grief, depression or excitement, also do not effect the continuous and consistent identification of one's personal self. A person can give up several of his interests and change some of his fundamental beliefs and social values or his religious tenets, yet, on that account, he will not feel that his I-identity was ever lost. Unlike the physical state, one can recall and relive almost all past experiences to their full emotional content. Thus, both the physical relaity and the psychic reality are variable in two different ways, but in between these two changing phenomena the I-identity remains as a constant.

When we examine the secret of this constant what we arrive at is a value which is in the form of an endearment. It is this value that is continuously perpetuating the I-consciousness as a stable nucleus of all the physical and psychic events that come to pass during the span of a life-

"This is what I like." One is committed to please one's own self with religious zeal. In fact, man cannot think of a greater torture than the thwarting of his prerogative to please himself. This is what the Guru terms here as *ātmagata priyam*, which means literally, "the endearment that goes toward the Self."

The *Kauṣītaki Upaniṣad* gives a picturesque analogy of the ascending path of man. As a being, man first enters into the world of physical reality where he derives sustenance from nature; the air becomes his vital breath, solar energy his fire, other thermal sources supply the body and the mind with energy for their growth and activity, and other friendly forces attend to man's needs like a shower of grace. Life moves on from moment to moment in a stream of timelessness. It grows like a tree and becomes the captive of its individuation. The will to live operates as an irresistible force called the *aparājita*. While the conscious life is controlled by the intellect, the elan vital is attended to by an autonomous system that is in charge of maintaining all bodily functions. It is placed between the potentials that are hidden away in a prior absence and the possibilities of the present into which one can mould oneself. In choosing one's part, one is endowed with the power of discrimination. The main sap of one's life is an abundant supply of libidinal energy. The spirit in man becomes wedded to two consorts: one is called *cakṣusi*, which means pertaining to the organs of perception, especially the eye, and the other, called *mānasi*, means pertaining to the mind.

Between the data provided by the senses and the preferences of the mind, the garland of life is woven until the body drops. In this analogy the individuating self also belongs to a timeless reality, and its will to live is none other than its will to love itself. In the same Upaniṣad there is another passage which says that the experiencing endearment is like the burning of the object of desire in the sacrificial fire of one's love for the Self; what persists in this process is only the resultant joy of love. The highest form of love is the love of truth and truth is none other than one's own Self.

The *Chāndogya Upaniṣad* associates the experience of endearment to the cosmic person's desire to enjoy. In the *Bhagavad Gita,* Arjuna has a cosmic vision during which he sees the countless mouths of the many as the mouth of the cosmic person, and all eyes, hands and legs as one person actively moving about to possess and enjoy the world that he desires.

In the *Brhadāraṇyaka Upaniṣad* it is said that it is not for the sake of the son that the son is loved, but for the sake of the happiness of the Self. The happiness of the Self is praised above everything else. In the Bible, though the object of desire is shown to be of no special worth when compared to the undiminishing value of the Self, another analogy amends this by saying that if a person who has one hundred sheep loses one, the love for the remaining ninety-nine will not compensate for the love he feels for the missing one. The endearment of the Self experienced on each occasion has its own unique quality.

Of all forms of joyous experience nothing surpasses the ecstasy that a couple derives from a fond embrace or an orgastic state, yet, even such ecstasy is surpassed by the peerless bliss of the Self, when the pure intellect of individuation, freed of all colourations, becomes united with the Self. When this happens one cannot tell if the consciousness belongs to a state of immanence or transcendence.

Verse 94

ulakavumuḷḷatumāykkalarnnu nilkkum-
nila valutāyoru nītikētitatrē
aṟutiyiṭān arutātavāṅmanō gō-
caramitil eṅṅu cariccitum pramāṇam.

The world and the truth exist intermixed;
this state is one of great iniquity;
in this, which is beyond the grasp of word and mind,
how can any right reason operate?

In our daily life the world appears to us as one whole piece belonging, all at once, to the same space and time. We do not realize how much the past, the present and the future are all interwoven. We visualize a uniform world. Part of this world is seen directly with our eyes and heard with our ears, and to that we add the recollections of what we have experienced at some other time, then this is further complemented by what we have heard or read as having been experienced by someone else. This picture is further enhanced by our imagination with the speculations of mythologies, theologians, and scientists.

The factual stuff occupies only a very small space of our visual and auditory range, and even this small area is beyond our physical range, as we have in our possession only certain sense impression. No one has yet proved that our sense impressions are exact copies of the models outside. In fact, if we are to believe the astronomers, the stars we see take us beyond several light years and thus the starry heaven is only the ghost of the past, which, however, goes pretty well with the panorama of our present. When a man in New York talks to a person in Bombay and to another in California within the time range of ten minutes, one man speaks to him from the past and another from the future. When we drive past the rows of trees of an apple orchard, the trees nearest to the car seem to move fast and the farthest ones more slowly, and so we see endless patterns of triangular formations, which give us a somewhat global vision in relation to an imaginary point that can be marked in the farthest reaches beyond the horizon. All these irrelevancies in time, space and appearance are ignored and such incongruity does not make us suffer in the least when our business is confined to a small physical area such as eating our breakfast or shaking hands with a friend. If, however, we become ambitious and attempt to execute a project involving large areas of space or long durations of time, then we have to leave the familiar ground of our physical notions and we must adopt many topological considerations.

The bargaining of prices in a flea market is comparatively easier than for two philosophers to convince each other of their respective stands. For example, when a Buddhist is asked to testify on a red pot and a blue jar, he will immediately raise an objection to the mixing up of names with things. According to him, pot, jar, red and blue are only arbitrarily devised names and actual things denoted by those names belong to another order of reality which can only be sensed. Sensations do not come in the form of names. When Aristotle or the Christian theologians make a dichotomy of an actual thing and its essence, the Buddhist thinks of this as a game of verbosity, since, in his opinion, perception happens only in the split moment in which the senses receive a stimulus from an object.

We see things not merely with our senses, but also with our mind. The mind is like a bombastic commentator who explains all impressions in terms of past experiences and future possibilities. Thus, all at once, perception changes into recognition and the mind attributes a use value to it, which originates from the intentionality of the mind to earmark an object for future use. We are very much deceived by the language we use. For example, when a Christian theologian says that a person is factually true because he belongs to the here and now world of perception and will essentially continue because he has an essence which is not confined to the fact, as a personal opinion it may sound innocent enough, but it can be vitiated with the ulterior motive of the church. If the basis of the reality is what is given here and now in terms of perceptual data, and as all that changes in a few hours or even after a split second, a person of the present cannot be accused of any of his past crimes. Yet, by accepting the concept of an unspent essence, the theologian can also maintain the essence of a man's sin along with the man's essence, and so the man can be called to account for his sin on the last day of judgement.

By mixing up the world of facts with the world of ideas, whether philosophically sound or fictitiously humorous, man can bring himself to situations of embarrassment, if not downright harassment. Narayana

Guru thus says that there is an inherent injustice in the peculiar mix-up of things, the responsibility of which cannot be put on anybody's shoulders.

Evidently there is an erroneous vision on the part of everyone. If all people should suffer from a disease which made everyone see all objects as doubles, there would be universal agreement in what is seen and consistency in their vision, but their perception would nevertheless be defective. All empirical knowledge is in the same position, and this kind of illusion is called *mukhya vibhrama.* If one person sees three moons when all others see two moons, he is making an empirical mistake and this is called *prātibhāsika bhrāntih.* As our experience bristles with such errors of both a transcendental and an empirical order, the Vedantins put in a category called "the cognition of the unutterable," *anirvacanīya khyāti.* The Guru, therefore, says that the reality of this world is beyond the comprehension of our mind. Both philosophers and scientists claim to have devices or methods by which they can give precise information of exact truths, but if we examine these claims in the light of what we have already said, it is not difficult to see that even the most ambitious scheme will have only partial credibility.

Verse 95

vipulatayārnna vinōda vidya māyā-
vyavahitayāy vilasunna viśva vīryyam
ivaḷ ivaḷ iṅṅavatīrṇṇayāyiṭum ta-
nnavayavamaṇḍakaṭāhakōṭiyākum.

This extensive playful display is *maya*'s
concealed energy of universal creativity;
again and again she manifests here; her limbs
are the ten million cosmic bodies.

There are many dialectical pairs of opposites, such as the transcendent and the immanent, spirit and matter, the eternal and the transient, the bright and the dark, the Self and the non-Self, the manifest and the unmanifest, wisdom and nescience, the timeless and the temporal, the vertical and the horizontal, the graceful and the obstructive. Between these pairs of opposites there is a fundamental paradox which needs to be understood by every contemplative in order to have a unitive vision of truth. This enigma or paradox that confronts the contemplative, causing a confusion which inevitably leads to misery, is the common lot of all, and we see fervent prayers offered in the scriptures of all religions for the redressal of this dark and deluding force.

In the *Īśāvāsya Upaniṣad* the prayer closes with a special request for the illuminating fire of wisdom to lead one from ignorance to wisdom and not into the crooked path of nescience. The Buddhists repeat at least five times every day their pledge of allegiance to the Buddha, the *dharma*, the *sangha* and the five pledges of restraint called *pañcaṣīla.* The Lord's Prayer says, "Lead us not into temptation," and similar prayers occur again and again in the Holy Quran.

What is treated as the devil or the dark deluding force by most religious believers is described by the Vedantins as *māyā*. In their hands, the connotation of this term attains to a philosophical magnitude which is not conceptually derogatory or despicable, as in references like the devil, *māra,* or *ibliss.*

Nataraja Guru gives the following working definition of *māyā* in his commentary on verse 54:

> *Māyā* is the principle of nescience or ignorance which is not an entity but a convenient term or mathematical factor or element with which to relate the two aspects of the Absolute which always co-exist. Like the square root of minus one and its positive counterpart in the square of the same number, understood reciprocally or ambivalently, as it enters into electro-magnetic calculations in modern physics, *māyā* is to be understood in terms of the philosophy of India, especially that of Śankara, as a negative vertical factor admitting contradiction horizontally but unity vertically.*

What is to be noted here is the special mention that *māyā,* when viewed vertically, can offer us a sense of unity and only gives us confusing multiplicity when it affects our understanding horizontally.

In verse 15, the concept of *māyā* was introduced as a drag in time. Boredom and anxiety are two evils that centre around a person's sense of time. Man is destined to sit and wait for long hours and sometimes years in vain anticipation of the arrival of a factual or imaginary moment of delight. In verse 19, *māyā* appears as the difference of opinion because of the possibility of the plurality of standpoints each mind can have, and it also comes as an obduracy which prevents a person from relieving himself of his vested interests and pet beliefs so as to have a more universal or catholic view. In verse 35, *māyā* is referred to as a veiling principle, which, like an appalling failure of memory, comes again and again even to a wise man so that he may forget the reality of his true Self. In verse 51, *māyā* is presented as the grand dichotomy which differentiates the subject from the object, and thus, in this context, it is the basis of the factual world of all transactions. In verse 54, *māyā* is the basis of the alternating phases of consciousness, such as the wakeful and the sleeping, which affects, with the alternation of day and night, not only human beings, but the entire world. In verse 57, *māyā* reappears as the potentials and the possibilities of a prior absence in the process of continuous actualization. As the incipient memories and the innate tendencies of man are also aspects of this process of actualization, man's destiny lies in his understanding of *māyā*. In verse 58, *māyā* is the most confounding confusion, which

* *One Hundred Verses of Self Instruction,* Gurukula Publishing House, p. 180.

breaks up the unity of all and pushes the mind into the prison walls of fragmentary interests. In verse 71, *māyā* is viewed vertically as a divine sport in which all beings have their assigned roles to play. The same verticalized view continues in verse 72, in which *māyā* no longer obstructs a wise person from having the most blessed experience of unitive understanding. In verse 87, *māyā* is given the exalted position of being as incomprehensible as the Absolute. However, in the next verse the reader is warned that *māyā* does not forgive even the slightest discrepancy of understanding and, in this context, it is identical with the unalterable laws of nature. In verse 94, the dark and bright aspects of *māyā* are dialectically paired and *māyā* is raised to an exalted degree of wonder. It is from this appraisal that we come to the present verse, in which *māyā* is given several bright epithets, even though it continues to be the vertical negative counterpart of the Absolute.

If liberation belongs to the science of the Absolute, our life on earth belongs to the science of the sportive humour of the cosmos. If God or the Absolute is presiding over one's liberation or emancipation, *māyā* presides over the ludicrous situations of trial and error and hide-and-seek of truth and falsehood. Unlike the domain of the Transcendent Being, the world of *māyā* is rich with a fecundity of manifestation. Out of nowhere, as though by magic, new bodies evolve and become animated with the most lively interests, but after playing a role which looks utterly serious, the manifested entities burst like a bubble and once again vanish into oblivion. The cause of laughter vanishes in the silence of gloom and depression, and the clouds of grief and despair are shattered by the brilliance of the beautiful display of the creative dynamics of life. Thus, on the whole, the comedy and the tragedy of life balance perfectly in *māyā*'s science of humour.

Verse 96

aṇuvumakhaṇḍavumasti nāstiyenni-
ṅṅane vilasunnirubhāgamāyi raṇṭum;
aṇayumanantaramasti nāstiyennī-
yanubhavavum nilayaṟṟu ninnupōkum.

The atom and the indivisible, both as being and non-being
shine from either side;
thereafter, being fades away
and the experience of non-being, having no foundation, will also
cease.

Our daily life is based on experiences coming from two sources; one set of experiences comes from our sensory perception and the other comes from our mind. The senses perceive particular objects and the mind places the particulars under categories and classifications which are formulated by general ideas. Consciousness oscillates between what is perceived and the general idea of a previous concept which enables the mind to identify what is perceived. Scientists, who are engaged in formulating general laws by resorting to the logical method of induction, go into the minute details of the particular by employing the technique of analysis and thus arrive at notions of atoms and their constituents such as subatomic particles. As all observations in science are to be referred to one unified principle, abstractions and generalizations are employed to give an integrated view of the total field of search. Thus, the world stands divided as the atomic and the universal, which the Guru terms here as *aṇu* (atomic) and *akhaṇḍam* (the indivisible).

The analytical and synthetical observations of the scientist are not different from the experiences of the common man who, in his day-to-day life, also relates himself to a number of particular interests .nd then goes to bold generalizations which, at least every now and then, release him from the bondage of objects, names and interests that are locally fixed. In this alternating shift of emphasis, the idea of the particular weakens the vision of the general and the vision of the general obviates the idea of the particular. The alternating interests of the particular and the universal seem to operate in turn in the mind in such a way that one pertains to the empirical world of things and the other to the conceptual world of subjective consciousness. The reality of a thing is not decided merely by its appearance, but by the interest, value, or meaning it registers in an individual's mind. To a hungry man the presence of food is intensely real, but to a fully satiated man it is something to be ignored. To a person who is in love with his wife or child nothing is more real than his wife or his child, but when he resents them they seem to become unreal to him. The main source of reality in one's empirical life is the need to satisfy desire and to avert fear.

In the *Bṛhadāranyaka Upaniṣad* (3.5.1) Kahola asks Yājñavalkya to explain to him the Brahman that is immediate and direct, the Self that is within all. To this Yājñavalkya replies, "This is your Self, that is within all." Kahola then asks, "Which is with all, Yājñavalkya?" and Yājñavalkya answers, "That which transcends hunger and thirst, grief, delusion, decay and death. Knowing this very Self, wise men renounce the desire for sons, for wealth and for the worlds, and resort to the mendicant's life. That which is the desire for sons is the desire for wealth, and that which is the desire for wealth is the desire for the worlds, for both these are but desires. Therefore, the knower of the Brahman becomes disgusted with scholarship and lives upon the strength which comes from pure knowledge. He becomes meditative. He discards what originates from ignorance and from scholarship and he enters into silence. By cancelling out what arises out of silence and non-silence, he becomes a knower of Brahman." This is what the Guru describes in this verse when he says that even this experience of being and non-being disappears.

We should bear in mind the implication of the terms "being" and "non-being." For a materialist or an empiricist the being is that which has an objective materiality, such as a cup of tea which he can directly perceive as well as sip to quench his thirst. To such a person the general notion of cups of tea appears to be a mere idea which belongs to the world of universals and thus, in this context, beingness is of the particular and non-beingness is of the universal. To a philosopher or to a quantum physicist the entire universe has its beingness in an indivisible reality and all the particular phenomena are only transient modes; In this context the particular is non-being and the universal alone has beingness. Whichever way beingness and non-beingness are understood, both lose their purport again and again according to the changing moods of the perceiver's mind. This can also be understood in another way.

According to the *Chāndogya Upaniṣad* and also to the *Bhagavad Gita*, the individual lives in two perishable worlds. One is the world where man produced gains by his efforts, but neither his tools, such as his body and mind, nor what he can produce, such as wealth, can last very long. The other world is the heaven he may merit by his good works, but the merit of good work is relative and eventually runs out, and the heaven that he might win is not everlasting. Thus, the world of here and that of the hereafter are equally transient. In the present verse Narayana Guru says that both our empirical experience and our conceptual experience, having no foundation, finally cease to be.

In the *Chāndogya Upaniṣad* it is said that a person might lavish his love on his father, mother, brother, sister, or other relatives and friends, and he might take delight in sensual pleasures like sexuality, or in music and other sublime sources of ecstasy. At the physical level all these items are of a perishing nature, yet, even when any of these items are physically removed from him, he can still hold fast to these values as the treasures of his heart. Heart in Sanskrit is called *hṛidaya,* which literally means "here it is." To some people their dead parents, wife, or children are insurmountable obsessions, thus the beingness or the non-beingness of these relatives does not prevent a mind from being affected by the sources of desire, hunger, fear and grief. These objects of interest are treated by the *Chāndogya Upaniṣad* as *anṛtam,* a malfunction that belongs to the nescience or negativity of the Self.

In the course of our daily life we are again and again relieved from the tyranny of ignorance when we go into deep sleep. In that state, both our beingness and non-beingness cease to be. Several passages in the Upaniṣads describe the content of deep sleep as *sat,* which means "pure existence." In the *Māṇḍūkya Upaniṣad* the state of deep sleep is described as an undifferentiated mass of pure consciousness, *prajñāna ghana.* We do not remain in deep sleep for long, so when we wake we come back to the world of being and non-being. The wise man, however, goes into the deep silence of his heart. In the *Bhagavad Gita* (verse 38, chapter 10) the greatest secret of the Self is described as a profound silence, and the austerity leading to such a state (verse 16, chapter 17) consists of restraining the mind from all its cravings and purifying one's creative imagination, so as to attain the cheerful disposition of serenity and gentleness with which one enters into a deep silence.

This verse is to be bracketed with the following one, as there we are given an elaboration of the final state to which a perfect contemplative goes.

Verse 97

aṇuvaṟivin mahimāvil angamillā-
taṇayumakhaṇḍavumannu pūrṇṇamākum;
anubhaviyātaṟivilakhaṇḍamam cid-
ghanamitu maunaghanāmṛtābdhiyākum.

The atom will disappear in the vastness of knowledge,
leaving no trace of its parts; on that day the indivisible will attain perfection;
without experiencing, one does not know this unbroken consciousness;
it is the silence-filled ocean of immortal bliss.

In verse 26 Narayana Guru describes the Self as the limb-owner which imprisons itself with a veil whose strands are none other than ignorance. In the present verse he introduces us to the final release of the finite to become once again identified with the infinite, the Absolute.

The *Aitarēya Upaniṣad* mentions the three successive births of the Self. At first the self is identified with a sperm that lies in the semen of a man and has the vigour and brightness (*tejas*) derived from all the limbs of the man. The sperm is an *aṇu* of microscopic stature. The archetype of the sperm is the cosmic person, ever-resting in the space of the symbolic heart of the divine song *gāyatri*, which has for its lower limbs the light (consciousness) that animates an embodied self, the vital fluids that circulate in the body, the nourishment that maintains the organism and the gross world that becomes the environment of the individuated self. (See *Chāndogya Upaniṣad*, 3.12.6). When the semen containing the sperm is transferred from a man to the womb of his woman, the self has its first birth, at that point it is both finite and limbless. The self is not created by anyone, it is born of itself, *ātma-bhūyah*. It becomes non-different from the organism of the woman, just like one of her own limbs; it does not injure her and she nourishes this Self of his that has entered into her. A question can be asked now, "Why does the self recreate itself again and again?" The answer given in the Upaniṣads is: *eṣa lokānā santayati*, for the purpose of continuing these worlds. In taking a body the self accepts two objectives: one is to envision the welfare of the world and the other is the contentment that can be derived from the fulfilment of this mission. These purposes, however, are not conducive to the emancipation of the Self. The woman subsequently gives birth to a baby with a well-structured body, which has in it all the vital organisms needed to live a full life on earth. This is the self's second birth.

Although seemingly born, the Self is unborn, and in principle it is independent; however, as a person fated to live on earth, its masculinity is vested with the understanding of all worldly transactions. He is a potential builder, always eager to engage in action. In his earthly life he is continuously exposed to needs, but he can overcome his hurdles and his life is even punctuated with short or long periods of joy and peace. He reasons, wills, acts and plays the forward game of life as one who will never be vanquished. He is heroic and he establishes his supremacy in the heavens, the atmosphere and on earth. The Self's femininity is intelligence and it has the power to modulate. She is aphrodisiac stead-fast, wilful and a fulfiller of the ordained. She gets into tortuous paths even though endowed with the quality of being elusive. She is both earthly in her designs and powerful in her words, she is the mother of all, an intoxicating wine of life, a provider of ecstasy-like honey and an initiator into the secrets of psychic powers.

After engaging in several actions of merit and demerit, facing both the prospects of fulfilment, *kṛtakṛtyata,* and of frustration, *nirāśa,* the Self finally wishes to be relieved of its bondages. Having reached his or her age, the person dies and the Self is born again. This is the third birth. In the *Aitareya Upaniṣad* (2.4.5), the sage Vamadeva speaks thus of these three births:

> Being yet in embryo, I knew well
> All the births of these gods!
> A hundred iron citadels confined me,
> And yet, a hawk with swiftness, forth I flew!

In embryo indeed thus lying, Vamadeva spoke in this wise. So he, knowing this, having ascended aloft from this separation from the body, obtained all desired in the heavenly world, and became immortal – yea, became (immortal)!

Although the Vedic poets cared very much for the hedonistic

pleasures of heaven, the later seers discredited this as of little value, and in the *Bhagavad Gita* Kṛṣṇa speaks derogatorily of those who desire the pleasures of the heavens. The highest goal praised by Vedanta is the ultimate emancipation of the Self, the release from the fear of death and the attainment of immortality

The following prayer is given in the *Bṛhadāraṇyaka Upaniṣad* (1.3.25)

asato mā sadgamaya
tamaso mā jyotirgamaya
mṛtyor mā amṛtamgamaya

From the unreal lead me to the real!
From darkness lead me to light!
From death lead me to immortality!

In this prayer the unreal (*asat*) is none other than death and the real (*sat*) is the same as immortality, just as darkness (*tamas*) is the same as death and the light (*jyotis*) is immortality.

The final emancipation of the Self is described in the *Bṛhadāraṇyaka Upaniṣad* in many striking verses of profound wisdom. In chapter 4, section 4, Yājñavalkya says:

5. But people say: "A person is made (not of acts, but) of desires only." (In reply to this I say:) As is his desire, such is his resolve; as is his resolve; such is the action he performs; what action (*karma*) he performs, that he procures for himself.
6. On this point there is this verse:
   Where one's mind is attached – the inner self
   Goes there to with action, being attached to it alone.
      Obtaining the end of his action,
      Whatever he does in this world,
      He comes again from that world
      To this world of action.
   – So the man who desires.
   Now the man who does not desire. – He who is without desire, who is freed from desire, whose desire is satisfied, whose desire is the Soul – his breaths do not depart. Being very Brahma, he goes to Brahma.
7. On this point there is this verse:

When are liberated all
The desires that lodge in one's heart
Then a mortal becomes immortal!
Therein he reaches Brahma!

As the stough of a snake lies on an ant-hill, dead, cast off, even so lies this body. But this incorporeal, immortal Life (*prāṇa*) is Brahma indeed, is light indeed.

This higher state is alluded to in this verse as bliss through and through. The *Chāndogya Upaniṣad* (3.5.4) describes the experiencing of the supreme teaching as one which produces as its essence great splendour, and it says: "Verily these are the essences of the essences, *amṛtasya-amṛtam.*"

The closing of this verse reminds one of the closing of Narayana Guru's Universal Prayer:

In the ocean of Your Glory
Of great profundity,
Let us all, together, become sunk
To dwell therein everlastingly in Happiness!"

Verse 98

ituvare nāmoru vastuviṅṅaṟiññī-
lati sukhamennaniśam kathikkayālē
mati mutalāyava māṟiyalumātmā
svatayaẓiyātaṟivennu colliṭēṇam.

We have not known anything here so far,
having spoken of great happiness;
even if intellect and such disappear,
the reality of the Self, without becoming disintegrated, will continue as knowledge.

In this verse the Guru says, "We have not known anything so far, having spoken of great happiness." It may sound strange to a person who has read or listened to 97 verses of Self-instruction to hear in the 98th that all his listening and meditating did not bear the fruit of knowledge. Knowledge in its highest sense is not different from being the Absolute. When a person says, "this is happiness," or "this is a greater happiness than the previous one," his knowledge belongs to a relativistic order. In absolute knowledge there is no approximation, either one knows or does not know. Even after knowing, if a person doubts his knowledge he is still in the dark. One should have absolute certitude in what one knows. This is illustrated in the *Chāndogya Upanisad* with the story of Satyakāma Jābāla.

Traditionally only a man of superior birth was accepted by a Vedic teacher to be initiated into the highest truth of the Absolute. The story of Satyakāma is given to illustrate the fact that the wisdom of the Absolute in unconditional.

Satyakāma was the son of a servant-maid and he did not know who his father was. He felt a great yearning to know the Absolute, so he asked his mother who his father was. She became sad and shame-facedly said to him, "I do not know this, my dear, of what family you are. In my youth, when I went about a great deal serving as a maid, I got you, but I do not know to what family you belong; however, I am Jābāla by name and you are Satyakāma by name, so you may speak of yourself as

Satyakāma Jābāla." Satyakāma went to see the Guru Gautama and asked for wisdom. In his innocence, he did not see any cause for shame in telling the Guru that he was illegitimate and born of a servant-maid. The veracity of the young boy's mind touched the truth-loving Guru and he received him as his pupil.

The boy was asked to take care of four hundred of the Guru's lean and weak cows. He took them to the forest and tended them till they became strong and had increased in number to one thousand. One day a bull in the herd offered to teach him a quarter of the Absolute. The bull instructed him to meditate on the east, the west, the south and the north, as the quarter of the Absolute known as "the shining" (*prakāśavān*). The Absolute is well-known to be of four quarters, or limbs. It is symbolized by *aum*. "A" represents the wakeful, or the eastern quarter where the sun rises, causing people to wake up. "U" represents the dreaming state, the western quarter, where the sun leaves man to his dreams. "M" is the deep sleep which is the southern quarter, the deep unconscious of the Alpha point wherein reside all the potentials to be actualized in the course of time. The three sounds, A, U, M are followed by silence, which represents the transcendental, or the Omega point, the northern quarter. Thus, what fills the four quarters is nothing but one consciousness. *Ākāśa* means "space" and *prakāśa* is the "light that fills the entire space." Satyakāma paid heed to the bull's instructions and honoured its words as though they were as respectable as those of God.

On his way back to the hermitage, he built a fire and sat by it. The fire suddenly spoke to him and offered to teach him a quarter of the Absolute. As Satyakāma agreed, the fire asked him to meditate on the earth, the atmosphere, the sky and the ocean, as the quarter of the Absolute known as "the endless" (*anantavān*). In the *Taittirīya Upaniṣad* (2.11) the Absolute is defined as *satyam, jñānam anantam brahman*, which means: "He who knows the Absolute as the real (*satya*), as knowledge (*jñāna*), and as the infinite (*ananta*) is the knower of the Absolute. One who knows the Absolute becomes the Absolute."

Satyakāma meditated on what the fire had taught him and on his way back to the hermitage he again built a fire and sat by it. This time a swan came to him and asked him to meditate on the fire, the sun, the moon and the lightning, as the quarter of the Absolute known as "the luminous" (*jyotiṣmān*). The Absolute is the light of all lights. Satyakāma meditated on this.

Before arriving at the hermitage, he once again built a fire and this time a diver bird came to teach him the last quarter of the Absolute. The bird told him to meditate on the breath, the eye, the ear and the mind. This quarter is known as *āyatanavān*, "the support of all." Satyakāma meditated on the Absolute as the ground of everything.

On arrival at the hermitage, his Guru saw him beaming with his inwardly gained light and asked him why he looked as brilliant as a knower of the Absolute. The Guru wanted to know if he had been instructed by someone and Satyakāma replied that he had not been instructed by any man, but only by the elementals and that he now desired to come to know the four quarters of Brahman from his Guru, as a disciple's knowledge does not become perfect until it has been learned from a preceptor. The Guru then taught Satyakāma the four quarters of the Absolute with its sixteen components, and this coincided absolutely with what the elementals had taught him.

The truth that permeates the world and the truth that comes from the word of the Guru are not two, however, when the conformity of both these becomes evident to a disciple, he feels fully assured that he has come to know everything. A person might be guided and controlled by the very Absolute itself, but until one knows that, it is as good as knowing nothing. In the *Bṛhadāraṇyaka Upaniṣad* (3.7) Yājñavalkya mentions how earth, water, fire, atmosphere, wind, sky, sun, the four quarters of heaven, the moon and stars, space, darkness, light, all things, breath, speech, eye, ear, soul, mind, skin, understanding, and the semen are all ignorant of Brahman, which rules over them all as the soul and the inner controller. Mere beingness is one thing, but to know one's beingness is another.

In this verse Narayana Guru attributes our ignorance to the comparisons we make of various degrees of happiness. Incomparable happiness is of the spirit, which is in the eye. In Sanskrit it is said, *sukha ākāśa akṣi puruṣa,* the happy domain of the person in the eye.

Supreme yoga comes only when the seer and the seen become united in one. In the case of an ordinary person, the eye sees everything separately and individually, but it cannot see itself. Such a person gathers information, but cannot claim to be a true knower because he does not know himself. When the world outside and the person inside become united in the act of seeing or knowing, nothing is left outside to be known and then alone can we say that we know everything.

Verse 99

arivahamennatu rantumekamamā-
varanamozinnavananyanuntu vādam
arivine vittahamanyamākumennā
larivineyinnariyānumārumilla.

Knowledge and I-consciousness—both are one
to him for whom the veil is removed; to another there is doubt;
if knowledge, having separated from "I," can become another,
there is no one here to know knowledge.

When I say "I am" and "this is" I am using the same faculty of consciousness to ideate both the subjective "I" and the object of my consciousness. As mentation is mostly done with the aid of words, there is a sequential order in which words present themselves to the mind. Because of the time factor involved in arranging thoughts, one may notice that the idea of "I am" is experienced as a separate event from the experiencing of "this is." On the basis of the semantic disparity which seems to exist between the many diverse components of consciousness, one may come to the conclusion that the self and its consciousness are separate. Truly, this is not so.

The tribasic division of consciousness, such as the knower, the knowledge, and the known, is a fundamental error which lingers in the mind of even the most erudite of scholars. In verse 14, the mark of a seer is seen in the one who goes beyond the boundaries of the three worlds with an awareness that shines with an all-filling effulgence, in which there is no semblance of any tribasic divisions of knowledge. It is hard to find such a wise person.

Although many people are theoretically convinced that there is only one Self and everything is a modulation of pure consciousness, they are still tempted to make a convenient divisions between the transcendental and the transactional. This is like having one norm for the church and another for the marketplace. The final test of wisdom comes when one is challenged to uphold one's absolutist vision without any compromise whatsoever.

The last vestige of *māyā* paints the Self as the sacred, sublime and mysterious that is not to be laid bare to the vulgarity of public gaze, and, in contrast to this, it caricatures the transactional as belonging to the mundane world, which can be the gross and commonplace where all profanities thrive. This kind of division caters to the shadowy world of charlatans, who indulge in conceit and self-deception.

To the truly wise, the sacred and the profane are relativistic ways of looking at one and the same reality of life. For such a person immanence is pregnant with transcendence through and through, and transcendence is a reality of the here and now. If such an absolutist vision of truth is not possible, then there is no point in speaking of an all-embracing Self that knows itself. The highest unity upheld by Vedanta is not a conjecture, but a truth in which the finite is woven into endless meanings.

Narayana Guru therefore says that the knowledge and the knower are not two. If, however, the knower gets carried away by the specifications of the name and the act of his knowledge, he loses comprehension of the unity of truth.

The seers of the Upaniṣads testify to the possibility of total knowledge when they proclaim without the least doubt: *Aham brahma asmi...* I am the Absolute. The *Bṛhadāraṇyaka Upaniṣad* (1.4.11) says:

> Whoever thus knows "I am Brahma!" becomes the All; even the gods have not power to prevent his becoming thus, for he becomes their self (*ātman*).

Verse 100

atumitumalla sadartthamallaham sa-
ccidamṛtamennu teḷiññu dhīraṇāyi
sadasaditi pratipattiyaṟṟu sattō-
miti mṛduvāy mṛduvāy amarnniṭēṇam.

Neither that, nor this, nor the meaning of existence am I,
but existence, consciousness, joy immortal; thus attaining clarity, emboldened,
discarding attachment to being and non-being,
one should gently, gently merge in *SAT-AUM.*

The Absolute cannot be termed as "that" or "this." A man recognizes his spontaneous awareness and he calls it "I." As this consciousness is self-founded and not depending on an external light, if he claims his ego to be the supreme Self, that is also not true.

The Self is the undeniable truth of everything. It gives room for the appearance of modifications and, within time spans, to evolutionary changes fully governed by appropriate laws, and for all gradations of values that can make immanence meaningful without negating the ever-transcendent reality of the one Absolute. When realization comes, disjunct, distinct, and relativistic orientations vanish and their place is taken by all-embracing knowledge, which is existentially self-founded and is permeated with the non-dual state that is glorified as immortal bliss. In this final stage individuation widens its horizon to infinity and becomes overwhelmed by the encompassing mystical union of all. The lone voice of the self merges in the vibrancy of *aum.* When this happens, let there be no resistance. May it come to pass.

AUM

[illegible]

[illegible] this, [illegible] the [illegible] existence [illegible]
but existing, consciousness, joy [illegible]
[illegible]
[illegible] to being and non-being.
[illegible]

The Absolute cannot be termed as that [illegible] man recognizes his spontaneous awareness and the [illegible] this [illegible] is self-founded and not depending on an external [illegible] claims [illegible] to be the [illegible] Self. That is also not true.

The Self is the unshakable reality of everything. It gives room for the appearance of manifestations and certain [illegible] forms [illegible] evolutionary changes fully governed by [illegible] law, and for all gradations of values that [illegible] without negating the ever-transcendent reality of the one absolute. When realization comes, distinct, definite and [illegible] pragmatic [illegible] and their place is taken by [illegible] which is essentially self-founded and [illegible] as immortal bliss. In this final state [illegible] and become [illegible] of all. The [illegible] When this happens, let there be no [illegible] that it [illegible] pass.

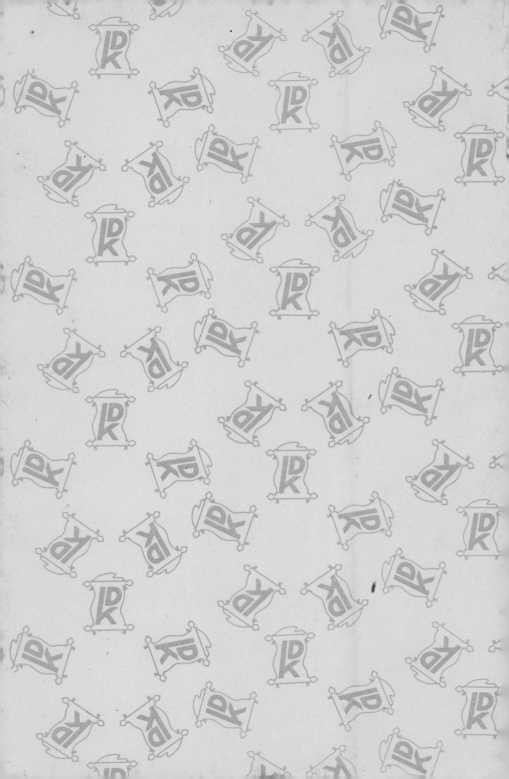